THE GIRL
from VENICE

Center Point
Large Print

Also by Martin Cruz Smith and available from Center Point Large Print:

Tatiana

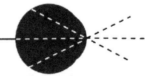

**This Large Print Book carries the
Seal of Approval of N.A.V.H.**

THE GIRL
from
VENICE

MARTIN CRUZ SMITH

CENTER POINT LARGE PRINT
THORNDIKE, MAINE

This Center Point Large Print edition
is published in the year 2017 by arrangement with
Simon & Schuster, Inc.

Copyright © 2016 by Titanic Productions.

This book is a work of fiction.
Any references to historical events, real people, or real
places are used fictitiously. Other names, characters,
places, and events are products of the author's
imagination, and any resemblance to actual events or
places or persons, living or dead, is entirely coincidental.

The text of this Large Print edition is unabridged.
In other aspects, this book may vary
from the original edition.
Printed in the United States of America
on permanent paper.
Set in 16-point Times New Roman type.

ISBN: 978-1-68324-229-1

Library of Congress Cataloging-in-Publication Data

Names: Smith, Martin Cruz, 1942–, author.
Title: The girl from Venice / Martin Cruz Smith.
Description: Center Point Large Print edition. | Thorndike, Maine :
Center Point Large Print, 2017.
Identifiers: LCCN 2016043667 | ISBN 9781683242291
    (hardcover : alk. paper)
Subjects: LCSH: Italy—History—German occupation, 1943-1945—
Fiction. | World War, 1939–1945—Italy—Fiction. | Large type books. |
GSAFD: Love stories. | Historical fiction. | Suspense fiction.
Classification: LCC PS3569.M5377 G57 2017 | DDC 813/.54—dc23
LC record available at https://lccn.loc.gov/2016043667

To Em from beginning to end

THE GIRL
from VENICE

I

Without a moon, small islands disappeared and Venice sank into the dark. Stars, however, were so brilliant that Cenzo felt drawn to them, even as mud oozed between his toes. The faint report of church bells carried over the lagoon, from farms drifted the smell of manure, and once or twice he caught the tremolo of a German gunboat plowing the water.

A curfew barred all nighttime activity, no exceptions except for fishermen. Fishermen were nocturnal creatures who slept by day and fished by night. They stayed out on the lagoon for days at a time and when they came ashore they smelled so much of fish that cats followed them through the streets.

Cenzo's only illumination was an oil lamp that hung on the mast, but he didn't need to see his catch; one touch told him whether he was handling sea bass, mullet, or a lost boot. He wore no shoes or boots himself; the mud would only suck them off. He did have a variety of nets and traps, tridents and rakes, for catching fish and damp sailcloth to cover them with. Every night was different. Tonight's catch was mainly cuttlefish come to lay their eggs. They rolled their otherworldly eyes toward the lamp. Fifty percent of fishermen said that cuttlefish were best caught on a full moon. Another fifty percent claimed the opposite. Sole, sea bass, and *orata* Cenzo laid in wicker baskets. Bullheads he threw back into the water.

The air reverberated as Allied bombers passed overhead on their way to rain destruction on Turin or Milan or Verona. Anywhere but Venice. Sacred Venice was attacked only by pigeons. The population of the city had tripled as refugees poured in, hidden by the blackout.

From the market Cenzo planned to sail home. For a week he had not bathed in freshwater or eaten more than grilled fish and polenta cakes. He pushed the boat off the grass to drop in the rudder when something sizable rose to the surface. Cenzo held his lamp over the water as the body of a girl took shape.

A chill ran through Cenzo. He expected any second that the girl would become a hallucination. Fishermen saw all sorts of things at sea and eyes played tricks at night. At a touch she might separate into the white belly of a ray and the blank face of an octopus. But no, she stayed intact.

She floated faceup in a dirty nightgown. He was no expert on the ages of girls but he guessed she was in her late teens. She was barefoot, her eyes were closed, and her skin was a nearly translucent white. Her lips were purple and long hair and sea grass wrapped around her neck. Cenzo was hardly a believer but he crossed himself automatically

10

and lifted her into the *Fatima*—no easy task, because the dead were so loose-limbed. Even as he laid her out on the bottom of the boat he knew that he should have left her alone. A woman on a boat was bad luck, and he supposed a dead girl was even worse.

Trouble he didn't need. On one side were Fascists, on the other side partisans, and on the third side German soldiers who would shoot you as soon as look at you. Only a madman would raise his hand and say, "Excuse me, *signori*, I found this dead girl floating by."

Still, Cenzo wondered how a girl had gotten so far from land. Granted, most of the lagoon was shallow, but its channels were labyrinths, and between channels and the push and pull of different currents a person was trapped as much as a fish in a net. Someone must have brought her this far and then, for whatever reason, abandoned her, although Cenzo did not see any bruises or signs of violence.

Cenzo untangled her hair. She had feathery black lashes and a small chin and with her closed eyes and youth she looked as serene as a Virgin in a painting. He couldn't throw her back as if she were trash. For decency's sake, he folded her hands over her breast and covered her with sailcloth he kept damp to cool the fish.

What to do? According to the Bible, the dead had to bury the dead and it was the business of the living to keep on living. All the same . . . all the same, there was something about the death of anyone young that was a slap in the face. He didn't count himself a virtuous man. In his experience, no survivor could. But he could compromise. In this blackness no one had seen him. He could deposit the body on the Ponte della Paglia in Venice, where the dead were displayed for identification, and still sell his catch before the fish market closed.

Enough! Decided! Cenzo stood facing forward, fit his oars into their locks, and rowed cross-handed, thrusting his entire body forward with each stroke. In a moment he found his rhythm and moved swiftly toward the margin between night and an abyss.

He deliberately did not speculate on the origins of the girl. A cruel father, a jealous lover, a suicidal impulse, insanity? Perhaps she was sent by the devil to lure honest fishermen to their doom. At the first tug of wind he ran up his sail, a sheet with the emblem of three cupids barely visible in the dark.

Fishermen believed in demons and wraiths. Everyone knew stories about men who took their place at the family table a day after they had drowned. Or of a miraculous vision of Saint Angelo that calmed a storm. Or of a captain who ignored a warning from the Madonna herself and was sucked by a whirlpool into the drink.

Superstitions. Fables. Bedtime stories to scare children.

He had barely passed from marsh to open water when the motor he had heard before returned, but much closer. A German gunboat was bearing down on him like a train and its spotlight crisply outlined him in white.

2

Bristling with machine guns on either side and on the bridge, the gunboat ruled the lagoon. The easygoing *Kameraden* originally stationed in Venice had been replaced by veterans of the Eastern Front, and the good cheer induced by early Wehrmacht victories had, by the spring of 1945, turned into the exhaustion of a losing war.

A soldier's brain was a simple thing. An ally fought by your side until the bitter end. He didn't quit in the middle of the war or need to be rescued or welcome your adversary with roses and wine. What was Mussolini now, il Duce or clown? And what were the Italians besides turncoats?

The soldiers threw a line to the *Fatima*, pulled it alongside, and gestured for Cenzo to drop his sail and cross over. They pushed him brusquely down into the well of the gunboat, where two SS officers in gray uniforms and jackboots studied a nautical chart by the glow of a hooded blackout lamp, because, while the gunboat ruled the lagoon, it was an insect compared to an Allied fighter plane. The older man seemed worn-out, while the younger exuded frustration. For dignity's sake, Cenzo plopped a shapeless hat on his head. Soldiers laughed at his bare feet.

"You are just the man we're looking for." The older officer motioned Cenzo closer. "You must help us settle a gentlemen's bet. Lieutenant Hoff is afraid we're lost."

The other officer protested. "No, Colonel Steiner. I was only expressing my opinion that we can't rely on local charts. We give people here too much credit. Fishing in a lagoon is like fishing in a barrel."

"Is that true?" the colonel asked Cenzo. "Is it just like fishing in a barrel?"

"Yes, but you have to know where the barrels are."

"Precisely. Hoff, you can learn something even from a simple fisherman. It's well-known that Italians are better at fishing than fighting. So I pose the question: Where are we?"

"How should I know?" the lieutenant said. "It's pitch-black."

The colonel looked up at Cenzo. "Can you point out on this chart where we are right now?"

There was no avoiding the colonel's gaze. One side of the man's face was ruined and gray and his ear was cut to a stub, but his eyes were bright blue and the impression he gave was of a noble bust that had fallen and been chipped but was still imposing.

The boat's engine continued to idle. Everyone turned toward Cenzo as if watching a dancing dog. The colonel said, "You must be eager to get to market. So show us on the chart where we are."

"I can't."

"Why not?"

"This chart is too small. We are farther north, at a marsh called San Spirito."

"Does it matter?" the lieutenant asked. "It's all one shitty swamp."

"If you don't know where you're headed, yes," said Cenzo.

Hoff's gaze had the smeared aspect of a drunk's. "Do you know why Italians fish on their hands and knees? Because it's the normal position for an Italian. Isn't that the way you fish?"

Cenzo shrugged. "It depends on the fish. Some you catch with a hook, some with a net, and some you have to get down and tickle under the chin."

"Lieutenant Hoff is new to the lagoon. Maybe you can give him a lesson," the colonel said.

"In what?" Cenzo asked.

"The simple pleasures," the colonel said.

"There are no pleasures for a soldier, apart from serving the Führer," Hoff said.

"Very correct. Do you hear that?" The colonel

raised his voice so that everyone on the boat heard him. He asked Cenzo, "Do you agree?"

"I don't know. I just fish. At night I fish and during the day I sleep."

"Alone?" Colonel Steiner said.

"Alone."

"And away from other fishing boats?"

"Wherever the fish are," Cenzo said.

"And tonight was like any other night?"

"Normal."

"You saw nothing, you heard nothing unusual?"

"I fish and I sleep. That's all."

"A simple life."

"Yes."

"Let me see your papers," the lieutenant said.

"I don't have them," Cenzo said.

"You're supposed to carry them at all times."

"I can't. They'd get wet and fall apart."

"You could be a partisan or a smuggler at the very least."

"Let me see your hands," the colonel told Cenzo.

Cenzo held them close to the lamp. They were thick with muscle and scars.

"The hands tell the true story of a person's occupation," the colonel said. "These are the hands of a fisherman. What's your name?"

"Innocenzo Vianello."

"To your friends?"

"Cenzo."

"From?"

"Pellestrina."

Hoff asked the colonel, "Where is that?"

"A village on the lagoon. Beyond the beyond."

It struck Cenzo that Steiner not only spoke Italian but even lapsed into Venetian dialect, which was virtually another language.

"I never heard of it," the lieutenant said.

"Of course. It happens that half the population in Pellestrina are called Vianello," Colonel Steiner said.

"I bow to your intimate knowledge of local customs," the lieutenant said, "but it seems to me, Colonel, that you are too forgiving to people who betrayed us. You sound as if you like Venice."

"I love Venice," Colonel Steiner said. "My family had a villa here on the Lido and my brothers and I spent our summers on the beach. Went to my first opera at La Fenice. Had my first love, a girl on the Lido in the cabana next to ours. After university, I studied architecture in Verona and Milan. How do you think it makes me feel to see the great temples of civilization reduced to rubble? You should see Rotterdam. Or Berlin. Go on, Vianello, get out of here. Get your fish to the market while you can."

The soldiers shifted out of Cenzo's way but Hoff was not finished. "Vianello, how old are you?"

"Twenty-eight."

"Then you must have served in the army. Where?"

17

"Abyssinia."

"Against natives with muskets and spears. You call that war?"

"It seemed like one."

Cenzo remembered mud-and-wattle houses pulverized to clouds of dust, black bodies covered with the suppurating sores of mustard gas, tanks that were immobilized by sand and no more use than teapots in a desert.

The lieutenant followed Cenzo to the rail. "Say you were an admiral and you discovered that a man aboard your ship was infected with the plague."

"I'm not an admiral and I don't have a ship."

"But say you did. Wouldn't it be your responsibility to the rest of the crew to isolate the infected person?"

"Probably."

"That is essentially the task that Colonel Steiner and I have been entrusted with. It is a sacred trust. Bring your boat closer."

"Why?"

"Because I ordered you to. Do you sail this boat alone?"

"Yes."

"That must be difficult."

"It should have two men but one will do."

"Let's see."

"You want to board my boat?"

"That's the idea."

Cenzo pulled the *Fatima*'s line and eased the fishing boat close as soldiers gathered at the rail. Cenzo had paid little attention to them in hopes they would do the same for him. Now their curiosity was piqued. An alcoholic fizz hung in the air. They had been drinking; he hadn't noticed that before. No help was coming from Colonel Steiner, who was now absorbed in his charts.

The *Fatima* nodded as Hoff stepped down into it. Under the beam of the lieutenant's flashlight, Cenzo lifted damp canvas from wooden boxes to display the astonished eyes of cuttlefish and boxes of sea bream and squid. The *Fatima*'s sail was furled and a card dedicated to the Virgin was nailed to the mast. The lieutenant spotlighted cigar boxes of hooks and needles, a trident and hand net, anchor and gaff, all leading to the sail-cloth piled inside the bow. The flashlight made hills and valleys out of the cloth's convolutions. What could be under it? A drunk, a dog, the body of a girl?

"If we're going to have a proper inspection, we're going to do this right," Hoff said.

He started with the boxes, not so much inspecting the cuttlefish as pouring them over the side and kicking in the crates.

The soldiers were entertained. Some tossed in suggestions of what the lieutenant should kick in next, like a test of skill at a country fair. Cenzo wondered how they would react when Hoff pulled back the canvas. That should make them drop their jaws. Then what?

Why had he picked up the girl? He had to be crazy. The trouble was the war. It should be over. Instead, the Americans were taking forever while Mussolini ruled a puppet state and the Germans, like decapitated ants, went on fighting.

"What's under the cloth?" Hoff asked.

"See for yourself."

Cenzo closed his eyes and imagined coming home to a parade of children and mewing cats. After a warm bath, sitting down to a dinner of melon draped with prosciutto, a creamy risotto with a pitcher of cold prosecco followed by osso bucco and a powerful red wine.

He didn't open his eyes until he heard Lieutenant Hoff say, "Typical pile of shit!"

In the flickering light, Cenzo saw cuttlefish that were stomped and exploded, broken crates, slashed nets, and sailcloth stabbed. There was no sign of the girl. He had not expected to see blood; the dead didn't bleed. But they didn't up and vanish into thin air either.

It took Cenzo a moment to realize that Lieutenant Hoff was quitting the *Fatima* and returning to the gunboat. From there the lieutenant enjoyed the satisfaction of a final order. "Get your boat out of here! It's a floating pigsty, a disgrace."

Cenzo rowed along the edge of the marsh. He

didn't know whether the gunboat would give chase, and by the time its spotlight swept the water, he had slipped into an opening too shallow for the gunboat to follow. Just in case, he kept his sail furled and moved the *Fatima* from one channel to another until the boat came to rest in a fast hold of reeds and grass.

He did a survey with his lamp. The damage on deck was not as bad as he had feared. He had lost a night's fishing and all his crates. His spear and rod had been snapped and would have to be replaced, but he could repair the nets and sailcloth. He even found the wrapped patty of polenta intact. When his inventory of the deck was finished, he went over the side and stood waist-deep in water with his lamp to retrieve a net tangled in the rudder.

What Cenzo didn't understand was the girl—who she was, where she had come from, and where she had gone. Maybe it was possible that soldiers on the gunboat had spirited her away while he was occupied with Colonel Steiner and Lieutenant Hoff.

Or was she a product of his imagination, the fantasy of a man who lived in a twilight world? Had anyone else seen this girl? Why hadn't Cenzo himself mentioned her to the Germans the instant he was on board the gunboat? It was not unusual for a fisherman who stared at the dark hour after hour to see a ghost in a wisp of fog or hear a soulful moan from wind passing over an open bottle.

A heavy drone made Cenzo look up as bombers—British Lancasters and American Liberators—returned in ragged formation from their night mission. Some were steady and aloof. Others whistled, their engines dying. One bomber in flames had the clamor and bright lights of a carnival ride, although no crewman on board could be alive. The fireball maintained a steady altitude and direction until it was out of sight.

Cenzo was waiting this war out. Abyssinia had been enough for him. Italy invaded a country that had an air force of one plane, and so, in a stroke, brought civilization to benighted natives and signaled the birth of a new Roman Empire. Every patriot was entitled to puff out his chest and thrust out his chin now that the Mediterranean was, once again, *Mare nostrum*. Our sea!

He came out of his reverie when something rocked the boat from the other side. He had been so pleased with himself for escaping the gunboat that he never considered the possibility that one of the Germans might have followed him.

He hauled himself onto the boat by his elbows, ready to attack. Instead he was face-to-face with the dead girl. She sat up and, without a blink, went back to consuming his polenta patty.

3

Cenzo knew the lagoon's hidden currents and channels, the deep sluices and semi-islands that appeared and disappeared with the tide, and he had hoped the girl was only a vision; yet here she was, licking her fingers and staring at him by the dim light of his lamp while she consumed the last of his polenta.

"Taste good?" Cenzo asked. "You're eating my supper too. Do you like it?"

The girl said nothing.

"What are you doing out here?" he asked.

Silence.

"What's your name?"

Not a word. That was all right. The less he knew about her, the better. She was like a fish that had flopped into his boat. What he had to do now was throw her back out. Maybe she would just vanish. It was unnatural the way she appeared and disappeared. He couldn't tell how old she was, anything from fifteen to twenty.

"I thought you were dead. Were you dead? Did you come back to life? You don't want to say? Have it your way. What I'm going to do is take you to the police. If you don't like that, you can always go back in the water."

He stood and pushed off with an oar to nudge

the *Fatima* through the reeds. It was a beautiful night, stars pouring down. The way sound carried over water, it was just as well she didn't want to talk. What he did not understand was how the girl had gotten so far from the mainland. The lagoon was shallow enough that a person could wade across much of it, but only by fighting currents going this way and that. The grasses, too, were a maze of channels that were waist-high one minute and underwater the next.

When he found a wind he raised the sail. The *Fatima* was about as fancy as a wooden clog, but its simplicity was its strength. It was designed with a high bow for bad weather and, for shallow water, a flat deck, no keel at all. Cenzo stole a glance and the girl combed out her hair with her fingers like a lady. He felt her twist around to get a sense of where she was. She wasn't afraid, he had to give her credit for that. But she still didn't give him an answer.

Sardines leapt into the boat and flopped around the deck. Volunteers, probably escaping a pike, Cenzo thought. Rather than slip on them, he tossed them back into the water. The girl stayed on her seat, an unwelcome but determined stowaway, her eyes steadily trained on him.

Cenzo didn't necessarily have a heart of stone. He took care of two families; people depended on him. He couldn't take chances. A month before, the body of a German soldier had washed up in the lagoon. The Germans simply lined up seven Italians and shot them dead.

Ahead was an ancient *lazzaretto*, an island where victims of the plague had been isolated, dumped, and burned. Not a pretty sideshow in Venice's history, but a perfectly suitable place to leave someone to be found and rescued, Cenzo thought, until he saw the gunboat as good as waiting for them at the island's dock.

The gunboat looked like a giant crustacean half out of the sea. On the upper deck, Lieutenant Hoff straddled the machine gun and sang in a romantic tenor, *"Wie einst, Lili Marleen."* Cenzo supposed it was no easy thing to maintain esprit de corps on the losing side of a long war, and a little carousing was to be expected. These were the troops of the walking dead. They had fought and lost at Anzio, had fought and lost at Monte Cassino, and they had seen enough fighting to know that, for them, the most likely end to this war was the grave.

Cenzo dropped sail and steered wide of the gunboat, but sheer momentum carried the *Fatima* into the mouth of a canal. The girl held him with a stare that made it plain she thought he had made a bargain with the Germans and was delivering her as agreed. She gave him a look that condemned him to hell and dove into the water.

Hoff climbed down from the gunboat, unbuttoned his trousers, and marched unsteadily into the dark to answer the call of nature. He pissed, shivered, and rose on tiptoe as he spied the girl climbing the bank. Patience was rewarded.

She clambered up the opposite bank to the paths and benches of an unkempt garden, driving a wave of rats from under a blanket of vines. A balustrade of marble and brick ran along the canal and she thought she saw faces move along the windows of the top floor. She pantomimed a call for help but all they did was shuffle forward in a dreamlike state. She pushed open a rusted door, stepped inside, and felt the sting of broken glass, then ducked as a white butterfly, like the beam of a flashlight, chased her down a hall.

"*Mein kleines Liebchen*, my sweetheart, do you know what this was?" Hoff asked. "A home for the mentally ill. But this island was also for quarantine, for carriers of the plague. They would be kept here to either get well or die. Usually die."

The girl crawled to a room meant for storage. What remained were headless saints, scavenged plumbing, and bats that fluttered in confusion. Meanwhile, Hoff played with his flashlight as if it were a watch on a fob. As he crossed the floor, his tone turned thoughtful, even philosophical.

"War has become too anonymous. There will be no odes written to today's heroes. No 'Horst Wessel Song' or 'The Charge of the Light Brigade.' Even in the camps, identity is reduced to a number tattooed on the arm. You should thank me for sparing you that indignity."

She crept into a courtyard gone wild with oleander and the flashlight's beam played hide-and-seek until she took cover behind a marble wellhead that was as tall as her chest and sculpted with the Winged Lion, the symbol of Venice. The beam bounced around courtyard tiles ever closer to the wellhead until the light shined directly in her eyes.

"Giulia," Lieutenant Hoff said. "We almost missed you. In fact, we had crossed you off the list, which would have been a great disappointment." He grabbed her by the hair, and when she kicked he held her at arm's length as if she were a trophy fish. "You will meet your father soon. Time is running out." The lieutenant found inspiration in the open mouth of the well. "Quarantine, naturally. That's the prescribed remedy for vermin."

But as he lifted her, his head whipped sideways. He staggered and turned to face Cenzo, who held a bloody iron pipe. The lieutenant had to laugh that anyone so inconsequential—an Italian, a bare-foot fisherman at that—would assault an SS officer. He dodged Cenzo's second swing and pulled the pipe from his hands. As Hoff unfastened the holster flap of a pistol, the girl bit his hand and the gun fell. He swiped her aside and stood wrestling with Cenzo as intimately as if in a dance, each choking the other while they kicked the gun and flashlight back and forth. Hoff won the gun but Cenzo picked up the iron pipe and hit the lieutenant flush across the forehead. The girl found the flashlight and aimed its beam into Hoff's eyes as they went opaque. An expression of disbelief, a general unraveling, passed over his face. Cenzo pushed the lieutenant and guided him over the lip of the wellhead to a momentary levitation, then to a plunge down the shaft and the sound of a muffled thud, followed by silence.

Cenzo gathered the gun, pipe, and flashlight and dropped them down the well after Lieutenant Hoff.

Shouting the lieutenant's name, Germans poked the dark with their flashlights as Cenzo and the girl moved from the courtyard to a garden. He carried her, because the soles of her feet were tender and his were tough. Besides, he had explored the island since he was a boy. He knew which paths were a maze and where artichoke plants grew to the size of men in armor and where wild goats shuffled in and out of olive trees. He took her on a switchback path that clung to the shadows until they reached the water. He put her down and they waded to the stern of the *Fatima*.

Cenzo assumed that some Germans were still aboard the gunboat. He had her hold on to the bowline while he slid the *Fatima* off the grass and pushed it toward open water. He stood and rowed two-handed, thrusting his whole body into each stroke, leaving wakes that were little more than swirls in the water. On the island, shouts faded, but Cenzo did not raise his sail until he and the girl were out of earshot and beyond the range of the gunboat's spotlight.

"The Germans won't find their friend in the dark right away, but they're very thorough. They'll find him. Then they'll come looking for you and me. So if you have someplace to go, now is the time to say so."

She was silent.

He said, "The German called you Giulia. Is that your name?" It was like trying to open a clam with bare fingers. "Giulia, why did the SS officer mention a list? What kind of list? A list of names? Jewish names?" She said nothing. "Perhaps you don't understand: compared to a gunboat, the *Fatima* is, well, not much faster than a cork. I find it hard to believe that your plan was simply to jump into the water."

She flinched when he moved toward her and draped his jacket over her shoulders. As long as she remained silent, she was a mystery. Cenzo couldn't claim to know anything about her, but he did know a little about the German SS. They only pursued two groups with the ferocity they showed against the girl Giulia: partisans and Jews. And people who helped them.

"Giulia?" he asked, but exhaustion had taken its toll, and she was fast asleep. He looked up at the coverlet of stars, the constellations that had comforted him when he was a boy.

When the girl awoke, the sky was bright and blue and the *Fatima* was approaching a scattering of weathered shacks that stood on stilts above the water. Cenzo's was the farthest from shore. He furled his sail, tied up to a pier, and urged her up a ladder.

The shack was built with enough oakum to caulk a boat, with makeshift portholes instead of windows and gaps in the floor that offered glimpses of water below. Rubber boots stood with a footlocker and laundry bag. Hardtack and cheese were suspended in a mesh bag out of the reach of rats. Nets were rolled in a corner. Orange crates had been turned into a desk with drawers for eating utensils, paper, string, and net needles. On one wall were hooks for clothing and on another was a painting of a fishing boat foundering in heavy seas. Lined up along the floor were jars of artist's brushes, a cigar box of paint tubes, turpentine, and a pallet smeared with color.

"You want to get out of those wet clothes." Cenzo threw her a dry salt-stiffened shirt and trousers and cut off a length of rope for her to use as a belt. He turned his back while she changed. He imagined what he looked like to her: some sort of wild man, half-dressed, hair in all directions, dark as an Indian.

"Now sit down." She reluctantly did as she was told and he examined the soles of her feet. They were more scratched than cut, light dues after a dash across broken glass. He hadn't studied her in the light before. She was imperious, with straight hair and a sharp chin. Cenzo conceded that the world she saw was a place where her name was on a list. The girl came with ghosts.

"Giulia, my name is Cenzo. My boat is the *Fatima* and this is my . . . palace, so to speak. The point is you'll be safe here if you stay out of sight. You understand the *Fatima* is damaged, so I need supplies and repairs. But collaborators and Fascists will be watching. I have to act normal and do whatever I usually do. I'll go to my mother's house, take a bath, go to the bar, play some cards. I'm sorry, but all that will take hours. Don't try anything silly like trying to swim across the lagoon. It can't be done. Most of all, don't touch the paints. So far I haven't seen the gunboat or any SS. But who knows? Maybe they haven't found the officer, and if they did find him, maybe they thought he was drunk enough to fall in the well. Maybe their boat ran out of fuel. Anything is possible. Hungry?"

He took down the cheese and carved her a slice. She maintained a suspicious eye on him as he located a bottle of grappa; it was homemade grappa and even the fumes took the breath away.

"Look, I don't know anything about this sort of business. I will try to help, but you have to be very careful. You hear about American pilots being rescued by partisans and led to safety? I've never met one of these heroes."

"Byron," she said.

He was taken by surprise. "Who?"

"Byron, the famous poet. He swam across the lagoon." Her voice was cracked from swallowing salty water.

"He did?"

"I want to go with you," she said.

"You can't and I won't be able to find any heroes for you if I stay here."

"Because you're not one?"

"Now you're getting the idea."

4

The fishing village of Pellestrina was squeezed between the lagoon on one side and the sea on the other. In between were simple two-story houses that leaned together almost close enough to touch. How could you expect otherwise from a community regularly engulfed by *acqua alta* in a grim battle against the sea. The rest of the village included a breakwater built by the Romans and a bunker built by the Wehrmacht. Saints precariously balanced on the cathedral roof were weary from watching the sea. At the southern end of the village was a bar and a shrine to Our Lady of Fatima, but the village was most animated by the fishing boats that shifted and creaked along its dock. Oriental eyes were painted on each bow and on the sails was each owner's fanciful emblem: a barking dog, a unicorn, a martyr set ablaze.

Two old fishermen sucked on their pipes and watched Cenzo spread his net across the pavers of the dock. Enrico and Salvatore Albano were so creased and browned by the sun that they could have been tree stumps.

"Your net is all torn. You got into a fight with a swordfish?" Enrico asked.

"You need a sword to fight a swordfish," Salvatore said. "You want to borrow my sword? It's rusty but it's ready for action."

"That sounds frightening. You might scare the swordfish to death," Cenzo said.

"*Touché!*" They could chew on that joke for an hour.

He left his sail for them to sew. The work afforded them loose change and something to talk about; they gossiped as much as old women and he knew what they said about him. He was Innocenzo Vianello, the man who wouldn't sleep with the most beautiful woman in Pellestrina.

He stopped at the marine shop to replace the broken oar, spear, buckets, and wooden boxes that Hoff had smashed. The next stop, more important, was Nido's bar.

The bar had no name except "Nido's." It had a long counter of mahogany, an espresso machine as big as a steam engine, and lukewarm bottles of wine, grappa, and liquors. A mural composed of seashells showed a map of Venice and the lagoon.

Nido's head was as smooth as a newel post. He had been a boxer and seen the world. On the wall hung photographs of him posing, fists up, with Georges Carpentier, Max Schmeling, and Primo Carnera.

"Poor Primo," Nido said. "I'm afraid he thought I had the evil eye."

"Why?" Cenzo loved Nido's boxing stories.

"I never told you this Primo story before. When America got into the war, Mussolini ordered up a newsreel that would show an Italian hero fighting an American Negro. They signed Primo as the Italian but they couldn't find a Negro boxer anywhere in Italy, so they settled for a North African. A musician, no less. They hired a couple of us to teach him how to throw a punch. At the bell, the musician ran out of his corner, threw one punch, and knocked Primo out. That's got to be the evil eye."

Salvatore and Enrico entered the bar and proceeded to the back, where there was a trellis of grapevines and outdoor tables. They joined a card game in progress with cards in hands oversized from fishing. Every once in a while someone announced "*Sette!*" for a winning score and "*Merda!*" for losing.

"It's not as if they spend money," Nido told

Cenzo. "I'd kick them out, but they're the most reliable business I have. Besides, where would they go?"

"You have a soft heart," Cenzo said.

The Albano brothers smirked and cackled to each other. They had played cards all their lives. It was, Cenzo thought, a race between seniority and senility.

"How about a grappa?" Salvatore asked.

Enrico's eyes became rheumy at the thought. "Very kind."

Salvatore shuffled back from the bar and smiled. A gap in his front teeth whistled where a gold tooth had been donated in the war drive.

"Swords are trump," Enrico said, and wagged his head back and forth.

"What are you thinking?" Nido asked Cenzo.

"I'm thinking that's me in thirty years."

"Ha!" Enrico said. "He's not so innocent, let me tell you that. He's got women coming and going."

"He has to dodge them like a bullfighter," Salvatore said.

"That Celestina has an ass like a Maserati," Enrico said.

"I forget, what is trump?" Salvatore asked.

"That Celestina," Enrico said with a beatific smile. "She's a regular *nonpareil*."

"How's the fishing?" Nido asked Cenzo.

"The Nazis were out early."

"On the lagoon? What were they after?"

"The devil knows. They trashed some gear and generally made a mess of the boat."

"And your catch?"

"Trashed that too."

"You've come to the right place. Not even the devil comes here." Nido poured a glass of wine for Cenzo and one for himself. "That's all?"

"I believe so."

Nido hunched over the counter. "I'll tell you what I heard. Last night the Germans raided the psychiatric hospital in San Clemente. Jews were hiding there and some of them tried to escape into the lagoon."

"They must have been pretty desperate."

"They must have been. Even the pope is trying to help them now. If you're a Jew waiting for the pope to help, it's too late, my friend, too late. Drink up."

The wine was sour enough to make Cenzo's eyes smart. For Nido, however, the liquor went down as smooth as silk. "When the Germans trashed your boat, you didn't resist or do anything foolish?"

"Not me."

"Good," Nido said. "Because I heard that last week a certain fisherman from Pellestrina, who sounded a lot like you, and a fish vendor from Venice, who sounded a lot like your friend Eusebio Russo, went to the cinema and, during the newsreels, shouted obscenities every time

Il Duce was on the screen. They say the two got the whole audience going. It was quite a scene. You wouldn't know anything about that?"

Actually, Cenzo and Russo had been drunk and all they shouted at Il Duce was "*idiota,*" which hardly counted as an obscenity.

"No," said Cenzo. "I've declared myself an official coward. I intend to outlive this war and the next."

In the mural on the bar's wall, Venice was a golden conch, the islands gilded limpets, and the Lido nothing but pipe shells. But without the Lido, would there be a Venice? Waves would roll in unhindered, flood the canals, and wash away the city that called itself La Serenissima: the Most Serene. What was Pellestrina? A mere cockle, a whelk. But without the fishermen of the Lido, what would Venetians eat?

"Did you hear anything else about the raid?" asked Cenzo.

"Well, they were after Jews, weren't they? That's the only thing that makes sense."

A figure in Fascist black entered the bar.

"I take it back," Nido said. "Sometimes the devil does come here."

Squadron Leader Farina placed a satchel on the counter. Farina was the village's leading Fascist, with a speculative eye that lit like a fly here, there, everywhere. He was accompanied by a pudgy boy in black shorts and a black ostrich plume hat.

"Cenzo, you're just the man I'm looking for. I'm signing you up," Farina said.

"For what?"

"What we talked about. Closing ranks. Do you want the women of Pellestrina to be violated by bestial Americans? Could any Italian man stand for that? You, in particular, should want to defend the Italian home and hearth."

"You think this is a good time?" Cenzo asked.

"It's the perfect time," Farina said. "You're a decorated veteran, a man of respect, and our German comrades have the enemy running back to Russia."

"If they're doing so well, why do they need me?"

"That's a defeatist attitude. Look at my son, a true Son of the She-Wolf." The Son of the She-Wolf wiped his nose with his cuff. "Umberto is only eleven years old and already knows how to operate a machine gun."

"He must be like his old man."

Farina said, "My nose is twitching. It's my sarcasm sniffer."

The squadron leader's frown worked itself to a semblance of good humor. "Cenzo, if you don't have the nerve to fight for your home, there are other ways to demonstrate your solidarity." Farina unbuckled his satchel and took out a newspaper that he opened to a page of advertisements for toothpaste, lipstick, trusses, vacations in the Tyrol.

"Take a look at this," Farina said. " 'Be a guest

worker in the Third Reich. Learn new skills. Learn German.' "

"I already have a skill," Cenzo said. "It's called fishing."

"See, only a coward would say that."

"Besides, I understand German tourism is flourishing. More trains are leaving all the time." Cenzo meant coffin trains. Both men knew it.

"Is that today's paper?" Nido interceded.

"Today's paper with an invitation from Germany."

Nido took the paper. "Good. What's playing at the cinema? It used to be pictures of elegant people with white telephones and feather boas, artistes like Mary Pickford and Garbo. What kind of actresses do we have now? German Gusils, Gretels, Elsies."

Farina reclaimed the newspaper and put it in his satchel. "Don't laugh. There will be a day of reckoning. Those who did not stand by Il Duce today will pay dearly tomorrow." The squadron leader thrust out his chin and pointed to the sky. "A new generation will redeem Italy."

"Yes, yes," Cenzo agreed. "In the meantime, I have a proposition."

"This should be rich."

"You know I'm a painter."

"An artist," Nido said.

"I wouldn't go that far," Cenzo said.

"Don't be modest. You have real talent," Nido said.

"Anyway," Cenzo said, "in their grief, people come to me to paint an ex-voto, a picture of their loved one's miraculous salvation or death, depending on the circumstances. You've seen them?"

"Everyone has see them," Farina said. "Get to the point."

"It's a very touching, emotional scene. The stormy waves or a child falling from a height and, above, the Virgin hovering, a glowing redemptive figure."

"So?" Farina asked.

"What if, instead of the Virgin, we had a different redemptive figure? I mean Il Duce."

"Instead of the Holy Virgin?"

"Exactly. There are photographs of Il Duce in every school and home and public building, but this would take him to a new dimension. No child, not even a Son of the She-Wolf, could sleep soundly without the protection of a sacred Il Duce. I could paint him over the Virgin."

"It's brilliant," Nido said.

Farina hardly knew whether to breathe. This was the kind of conversation that could get a man shot. Or promoted. In slow motion, he grabbed Umberto and steered him out the door. As soon as the father and son were gone, Nido whistled and said, "Thin ice, my friend, very thin ice. Remember, even a worm has teeth."

"What about you?"

"I'm too old to bother with. Besides, if they ever shut down this bar, there would be a genuine rebellion. Stay for a minute. I have another Primo story for you."

"Tell me."

"Some friends and I went to New York to help Primo train for his big fight with Max Baer. It turned out we were almost pallbearers. Primo was knocked down eleven times and each time we told him, 'Stay down!' He was just an 'Ugly Mug from Udine' but he had heart."

"What are you trying to tell me?"

"I'm telling you to stay down."

From the bar, Cenzo went to his mother's house. For him not to visit his mother and, incidentally, deliver his laundry would have caused comment.

Sofia Vianello was up on the roof, hanging sheets to dry, when he arrived. She was a small woman dressed in black. In fact, all the women of Pellestrina wore black, because they had all lost a husband or a brother or a son. All the men in the village had black armbands sewn onto their jacket sleeves.

He was a week early and at his sudden appearance she expected the worst. "What happened? Has something happened to the boat?"

"Nothing. I tore my nets."

"On what?"

"I don't know. Something underwater."

"Hugo never tore his nets."

"My brother was perfect."

"I'll tell Celestina you're here."

"Please don't bother her. I'm only going to be here for a second."

"No bother. She will be upset if she doesn't see you." His mother leaned from the roof and shouted to the house next door, "Celestina! Guess who's here!"

"Don't. I have to be going."

"Nonsense. You have to eat something before you go. Celestina!"

He heard footsteps on the stairs and someone battling through the sheets.

"Isn't she beautiful?" his mother asked.

Celestina was. Even in mourning, everything about her was heaving and buxom, with a healthy olive complexion and long, black stockings that begged to be unrolled. It was customary in the village for an unmarried man to marry the widow of his brother, in this case Hugo, a deed that seemed overdue. Celestina certainly seemed willing, and yet, Cenzo was numb to her attractions.

"Are you all right? Did something happen?" Celestina asked.

"Nothing. I was just telling my mother there was a little problem with the nets. I knew if someone saw me on the dock and told her that she would worry."

"He was hoping to see you," his mother told Celestina.

"No," Celestina protested. "There are lots of girls in Pellestrina."

"Only one like you. Isn't that right, Cenzo?"

"I think he only came to have his laundry done." Although Celestina laughed, a note of panic crept in. As she had said, there were many girls in Pellestrina, and few marriageable men, and Cenzo, the prime candidate, was mysteriously elusive.

"I could use something to eat," he said. "And maybe some food to take back to the boat."

"I made minestrone," Celestina said, and retreated down the stairs.

She laid a bowl of soup and a slab of bread on the kitchen table.

"I'm going to leave now. I know that you and your mother want to talk."

While Cenzo ate, Sofia's gaze zeroed in.

"What's the matter with you? First you lose your own woman. Now you spurn your brother's? You're lucky to have a second chance."

"This is good soup. Where did you get the beans?"

"Forget the beans. Think of the family."

"I support our family. I'm not as rich as some, but I help."

"I don't mean money. She's too young to be alone. If it comes to that, Innocenzo, you're too young to be without a woman."

"You and I have a deal. I will marry when the war is over. I thought we agreed to that."

"That's when I thought the war was almost over. Before Il Duce, may he roast in hell, and Hitler, may they roast together, decided to fight on. It's been more than four years now. This war may never end."

"Celestina is a beautiful woman. If someone else proposes to her in the meantime, I won't stand in their way."

"You're impossible. Name one flaw in Celestina."

"I can't. She could make a sausage stand up and whistle."

"That's because she always does the right thing. She's not one of those women who suddenly change their mind and pop up or disappear. You've had the last of that sort, I hope."

He was ashamed of the way he treated Celestina, but the more she tried to please, the more distant he became. It was her predictability that kept him at arm's length. There wasn't a word she said or a gesture she made that he couldn't anticipate. He could live with that for a day, but could he stand a lifetime of deadness, when every touch of the hand or batting of the eyelashes was mechanical? It wasn't anything he could blame her for. She was sincere and that should have been enough.

Cenzo mopped up the last of his soup with bread and pushed back his chair. "I have to get back to the boat. But there is one other thing. Do you have any extra blankets?"

"Now, why would you need extra blankets? You have a bed right here."

"Never mind, I'll sleep in the cold."

"You're impossible."

He was impossible. A coward and cuckold. A shipwreck.

5

He climbed the ladder and found the girl huddled in a corner of the shack with a boning knife in her hand.

"Food." He opened a duffel bag and brought out sacks filled with sausage, dried peas, dried beans, dried fish, biscuits, olive oil, and wine. "Not bad, huh? And fried polenta. I know that you like that."

"Why did you take so long? I thought maybe you were turning me over to the Germans."

"How can you say something like that?"

"Most people would."

"Well, I wouldn't. I told you, I had to act like it was a normal day. Normally, after some crazy SS officer tears up my gear, I have to go to the dock for repairs. When people see me on the dock, they expect me to go to the bar of my friend Nido, and I certainly can't visit him without seeing my mother."

"That's all?"

"That's all. So relax. I thought of an old friend

who can help." He put out his hand but she would not surrender the knife. Drying out had brought about some changes. Her hair had become a black mass of curls and her eyes brimmed with burning accusation.

"Isn't that good of you," she said. "You left me here in this hovel while you spent the day drinking with your friends."

"It's not a hovel."

"To the untrained eye it is."

"I told you, I have to act normally. First, I'm going to eat. Eat, fish, sleep, eat, fish, sleep. That's a fisherman's life."

"But—"

"Like I said, I'll try. See, I brought blankets from home and I bought you a shirt and pants more your size." He offered them as a gift.

She regarded them with disdain.

He said, "You may have noticed that Pellestrina is not a fashion center."

"Turn around."

"Why? Oh." He did as ordered while she changed. She had barely escaped with her life. He wanted to be fair and understanding, but he couldn't help but notice that items in the shack—boots, hat, footlocker—had shifted. "You've been looking around."

"No I wasn't."

"Did you stay away from the windows?"

"Those aren't windows, they're peepholes.

Nobody saw me, if that's what you're worried about."

There were a lot of things he could tell the girl not to do, like whistle on deck or ship an oar the wrong way round, but she would be gone soon enough and he was not teaching any classes on fishing or seamanship. He had no curiosity as to her history or family, likes or dislikes. She was from Venice and he was from Pellestrina, which was like saying they were not only from opposite sides of the lagoon but from different worlds. When she spoke she had an elegantly lazy Venetian accent. When he spoke, consonants disappeared. He decided she looked exactly like what she was, a girl in the costume of a fisherman. She would fool nobody.

"How old are you?" he asked.

"Eighteen."

"Really?" He looked at her with curiosity. She was a little bird whose eyes could light a room.

"Staring is rude," she said.

"Sorry. We don't have that many people resurrected at this end of the lagoon."

"I doubt you have many people at this end of the lagoon at all."

No, not a bird. She was like a hedgehog ready to bristle at the slightest touch.

She devoured a sandwich of ham and provolone and drank half a liter of water. When she was finished he asked, "So you know the Lido?"

"Of course. I've been coming here all my life."

"Tell me what you know."

"Everything. We have a house in Venice and a cabana on the Lido. We always went to the Excelsior Hotel and the casino."

That was what he thought. She didn't know the lagoon, its marshes, or its fishing villages. She probably couldn't find Pellestrina on a map.

"What was your plan? Where were you headed?"

"My father said to go south until I found the American army."

"Well, a lot of people have been waiting for the Americans. What would you do if you found them?"

"I'd tell them who I am."

"Who are you?"

She didn't say.

"So you would find the Americans. Do you speak English?"

"Obviously. Why else would I try to find them?"

"Anything else?"

"French."

"You seem educated. Your family must be well-off. French here, cabanas there."

She sat up stiffly. "I can pay you later. What do you want?"

"I don't want anything from you. You think I'm doing this for money? You know, you are very insulting."

"I don't want to owe you."

"Well, you do. You owe me your life. What's your life worth?" Aha, he had scored one palpable hit with that and brought a tear to her eye. Instantly, he regretted it. But she was a moving target, one moment a Joan of Arc, the next moment a vulnerable girl. "I heard that last night the Nazis rounded up Jews hiding in the hospital on San Clemente. Was that you? Were your father and mother with you?"

"I don't know."

"You don't know? The SS officer even knew your name was Giulia."

She shrugged.

"Okay, you win. I get more information from a dead German than from you and you expect me to risk my neck. I'll do it, but just to get rid of you."

"It's a common enough name around the world. Have you ever been off the island?"

"Yes."

He had Mussolini to thank for that. The war in Africa had demanded all sorts of skills. Men who had only fished or pushed a plow learned how to fire artillery or drive a tank. Or, if their tank was hit by enemy fire, how to turn from a human being into a can of jellied fat.

In Ethiopia, Cenzo had piloted a reconnaissance plane. It was like being the thumb of God to drop a round out of the sky onto some black heathens. Cenzo drew the line, however, at poison gas. He and his copilot should have been shot for refusing to follow orders, although what was the difference between blowing up some poor bastard with TNT and burning him alive with gas? As punishment, they were given the duty of bulldozing dead natives into mass graves and given dishonorable discharges that they considered superior to campaign medals.

She asked, "So you thought of someone in Venice or the Lido who can help?"

"Maybe." He wasn't going to divulge his old copilot's name, but the man was a regular Garibaldi, the kind of larger-than-life hero who a girl could pin her hopes on.

"Thank you."

"You're welcome." He had been wondering when she would find the words.

"When do you think we can go?"

"The sooner the better." That didn't sound exactly the way he wanted.

She said, "You must be eager to get me off your hands."

"It would be better for all concerned."

"The less you know . . ."

"That would be better too."

He could feel her searching for a neutral topic. For his part, he considered fish, boats, Mercurochrome.

"What do you do when you go to a bar?" she asked.

"Drink."

"Besides going to the bar, what else do you do?"

"Mend nets."

"So, when you meet your friends, what do you talk about?"

"The weather. Weather is important to a fisherman."

"Do you mind if I sleep a little?"

"No."

"We will have a pact of silence," she said.

"Agreed."

She spread out on the new blankets. He could tell that she wasn't sleeping, only excusing herself and him from the burden of conversation.

"Personally, I hate the poetry of D'Annunzio," she blurted out.

He wondered where that came from.

He did some calculations. She spoke French, English, and Italian. Italian education was more concerned with basic literacy than foreign languages, and there might be instruction in a second language at a private school. But to master three languages? That smacked of a private tutor. And if her family had retreated behind garden walls when the racial laws were instituted in 1938 and gone into hiding when the roundup of the Jews actively began in 1943, she had been sheltered for the better part of five years. That would explain her reticence. And was that perhaps why she acted and looked so much like a young girl? As if she had not been allowed to grow.

· · ·

Sometimes it was anchovies or bream that ran. Tonight it was cuttlefish that swam under the *Fatima* as soon as the boat sailed away from the shack. Cenzo thought a man with a large enough lamp could lead them like an orchestra conductor. Above, the nightly British bombing had begun, the engines of the planes sparking and throbbing on their way to Turin or Milan.

"Do they ever bomb fishing boats?" Giulia asked.

"Sometimes. If you see any fighters approach, stay low."

She stayed defiantly upright. "You have some decent books in your footlocker and some nice folk art."

"Those paintings are not folk art and I'm not illiterate. Please don't go in there again."

"Did I tell you about Byron?"

"You told me. Was he a good fisherman?"

"I don't know."

"So we're even."

"That's ridiculous. Byron was a poet."

"You must be getting tired."

"Of what?"

"Talking."

She recited, " 'He sinks into thy depths with bubbling groan, / Without a grave, unknell'd, uncoffin'd and unknown.' "

"That's cheery," he said.

Cenzo did not want to hear poetry; he simply wanted to hand her over like any other contraband smuggled on the black market. If he could unload her tonight, he would do it. As long as Eusebio Russo was at his usual stall at the Rialto fish market, the transfer should be simple. Russo was an accomplished smuggler, a master of sleight of hand whether it came to Spam or cigarettes. And if Russo couldn't do it, he'd know who could.

The sea was calm, reflecting a three-quarter moon that lured fish and fishing boats from the ports of Pellestrina, Malamocco, and Burano. Each boat had its territory and black stakes led the way to rows of shellfish ready to be plucked.

"Remember, I can swim," she whispered.

"And hold your breath and play dead. Can you do that again?"

"Why?"

"We may run into Germans again and they will be suspicious if a fishing boat doesn't have any fish."

"So?"

"So we're going to catch some fish."

"How?"

"Can you hold the lamp steady?"

He had her hold the oil lamp low enough for its glow to filter through brackish water full of floating matter, the tiny particulates of life. A spiral net brimmed with sardines as bright and blue as knife blades swimming round and round.

Cenzo swung the net out of the water and poured fish into the boat.

"It's your job to cover them with sailcloth to keep them wet."

"Why?"

"Just do it." It was like towing Cleopatra on a barge, he thought.

"That's it? That's all there is to fishing?"

"Pretty much, as long as you know where the fish are. So, tonight you are a fisherman." He scooped up mud and dirtied her face. He didn't want her pale cheeks giving them away.

Fishing was more a matter of tending nets than hooking a fish. For Cenzo, hours in a boat always passed quickly. He had enjoyed the work ever since he had been a *putto di mare* born to the sea. His father had hoped for three *putti*, but the Allies had gunned down one son and fame had seduced another. Now there was only Cenzo.

That the girl regarded fishing as low or demeaning hardly bothered him. He thought fish were mysterious, more a race than a species, and an invitation to another world. If she didn't see it that way, it was her loss.

The girl was a brief interruption in his life and the less he knew about her, the better.

"It's not like it used to be," he said. "The curfew has shut down a lot of restaurants, but it keeps us busy, doesn't it? All right." He motioned Giulia to take cover as they approached the market.

Venice was shaped like a fish and the Rialto fish market was its gullet. Although the city was in blackout, lights and waterborne jostling grew as boats maneuvered for the approach to the dock. He motioned Giulia to take cover. A second wave of bombers passed overhead on their nighttime run, regular as celestial clockwork.

Suddenly, market stalls appeared ahead. They were hung with enough lamps to display not only cuttlefish but translucent squid, silvery anchovies, cockeyed sole, lobsters green as jade, and ruby-red slabs of tuna, everything that the sea could give birth to.

Marble columns stood between heaps of whelks and cockles. Transactions were carried out on stone pavers shining with slime.

With a single long oar Cenzo punted the *Fatima* against the dock. "Stay under the sails," he told Giulia.

"Am I safe?"

"If you can stand being quiet."

Above, dawn turned clouds into puffs of color.

Cenzo found his friend Russo's stall but Eusebio Russo was gone. His stall was empty, pasted over with a stencil of Mussolini and the message "Be Loyal!"

Like a man desperately shuffling cards, Cenzo considered other possibilities. As soon as he sold his catch, he moved the *Fatima* into the shadow of the Rialto and entered the church of San Giacometto.

The confessional of the church kept fisherman's hours. As Cenzo stepped into the box, he felt weight shift on the other side of the curtain and smelled cigarette smoke.

"What happened to the fishmonger Russo?" he asked.

"He was a troublemaker. A communist. Are you a friend of his?"

"He owes me money."

"I doubt you'll see it."

It had been a while between confessions for Cenzo, but, as he remembered, a priest usually began by asking how long it had been since a person's last confession. Just by its smell, Cenzo could tell that the priest smoked a "Juno," a paper tube half filled with raw tobacco. Cenzo remem-bered the advertisement: "Berlin Smokes Junos!" He slipped out of the booth and made room for an old woman who looked eager to recite a litany of sins.

Daylight began to slide down the top floors of palazzos. The Rialto revealed itself in a crepuscular fashion from ghostly to real. A priest rushed out the church doors and scanned traffic in each direction but was confused by the constant interweaving of fishing boats, fireboats, gondolas, ferries, and barges of coal while Cenzo, standing in the *Fatima*, rowed cross-handed with two oars under the bridge into the golden dawn of the Grand Canal.

6

Cenzo felt that some people, like the Count of Monte Cristo, had the good fortune to be imprisoned with a benefactor. Giulia, obviously, was marooned with an idiot. He tried to think of anyone besides Russo able to smuggle a girl out of Venice. Unfortunately, smugglers were not trustworthy individuals. He had heard about partisans leading downed Allied pilots to safety. Except for Russo, the partisans who Cenzo knew tended to be chicken thieves.

In the meantime, Giulia curled up in a corner of the shack and refused to eat or drink. She was skinny to begin with and now she seemed determined to waste away from disappointment.

"I'm sorry my friend wasn't there," he said. "It seems like he was arrested by the Fascists before we got to the market. Bad luck."

Daytime was sleep time for fishermen, but Cenzo stayed awake in case the girl threw herself overboard. He felt the cool breath of rain on its way; he had a built-in barometer when it came to the weather. A light patter on the roof of the hut might be perfect company for a nap, but it was not a luxury he and the girl could afford, not both at the same time.

"You go to sleep," Cenzo said. "I'll let you know if anyone is coming."

"Would anyone come?"

"Not really."

Cenzo cupped his cigarette and watched through an open slat as rows of whitecaps marched across the lagoon. People drowned. His younger brother Hugo never learned how to swim. Some fishermen were like that, as if knowing how to swim invited the necessity.

A few fishing boats headed to the dock for new nets or a change of gear. Some fishermen he knew by their sails, like Scarpa's *Barking Dog*, Zennaro's *Panther*, and Busetto's *Unicorn*. He saw no pleasure boats at all. To fishermen, people with yachts barely scratched the surface of the water. Fishermen were rough-and-tumble. Rich boys posed. He could imagine Giulia on the fashionable end of the Lido among the hotel cabanas and Hollywood movie stars. Waiters carried cool drinks across the beach and small planes towed banners celebrating Cinzano. Not now, of course. Movie stars didn't come to the Lido anymore.

Death was fickle. Although the Germans must have found Lieutenant Hoff's body by now, they had not taken the customary Italian lives in return. At the same time, Russo had been plucked out of the fish market and replaced by a poster of Il Duce. Nets were more predictable.

Every net, no matter what size or configuration, ended in what fishermen called a "death chamber." This was the place of no escape, where fish swam round and round and went nowhere.

He sat against the wall and closed his eyes.

How did the girl get so far into the lagoon? That was where her story didn't add up. If she was so wealthy, why hadn't her family bought their way out of Venice? If her father was so smart, why did he wait so long? She herself was thoroughly brave. Cenzo gave her that much.

He was startled awake by the sound of heavy pounding and moved to the window. The rain had become a squall that turned the lagoon black and made the hut shudder on its legs. As the storm gathered in intensity, wind whistled through the floor planks. The *Fatima* was tied to pilings under the hut fore and aft. Craft at sea would head into the wind. In a fisherman's hut there was nothing to do but listen to the boards twist and groan. The girl still slept; that was the gift of youth. He looked at the girl's hands and saw how delicate they were. His hands would end up looking like claws shaped by the constant pulling on oars and wrestling with lines. No wonder he was such a crude example of mankind.

For a moment there was an eerie silence and then a soft thud as the boat nudged the hut. The second thud was harder. He went out onto the deck of the shack and stopped. The anchor line had snapped and the *Fatima* had moved ninety degrees away from the ladder. As the wind picked up, the boat gathered strength and swung with more abandon into the pilings that supported the hut. This was not as God intended, Cenzo thought. Boxes and gear shot like shuttlecocks around the *Fatima*'s deck and left no space to jump to. He needed to get on board, but every time he prepared to jump, the boat pitched and boxes slammed against the mast.

A newly bought oar was on the deck of the fishing hut. He used it to slow the boat's momentum but the blade broke off and flew into the air. Cenzo plunged into water that was waist-high one moment and over his head the next, dragging him one way and then the other.

He looked up to see, like an apparition of the Virgin, Giulia on the deck of the shack. When she disappeared he assumed that she had been swept away. Between the waves and rain, he could barely stay afloat. Just when he thought she was lost, she reappeared with a rope. One end she tied to the rail, then tossed the other in his direction so it uncoiled as it flew. He caught the rope, tied it to the boat's forward cleat, half swam and half waded with it to the nearest channel marker, and tied the rope to that, first slackly and then tight.

Giulia heaved another rope high into the wind so that it carried to the second marker. He tied up that line and released the first, which he carried to the third marker, in essence walking the boat around the hut to the leeward side, where it was sheltered, not beaten by the wind.

And then the storm was over. It moved on like a black locomotive headed to another station. He climbed the ladder and found Giulia in the shack, devouring polenta.

"In my first storm at sea, I was petrified, Cenzo said. "The waves were so high I thought the sea was upside down. I was six years old."

"That young?"

"I wanted a shirt. I didn't have one and my father said I would have to earn it. That was the day I started to work on his boat. Not this one but a bigger one. Cleaning the deck, mending nets, fetching cigarettes and coffee. He never explained anything. He would just do and I would watch. He was king. From one end of the lagoon to the other, he knew more good places to set a net. Other men wanted to work for him because he always found fish. He used to wake up first and open the sails and kids would come tumbling out. My family name is Vianello but my brothers and I were called *putti di mare*."

"What a beautiful way to wake up. Like a fairy tale."

"It sounds that way, doesn't it?"

In a loose shirt and pants she looked like an underfed boy, although she stuffed herself with polenta and ham and gulped water from a bottle wrapped in straw. It had taken them hours to sort out the boat. They had not been aware when night fell and now only the faint light of a hanging lamp lapped the interior of the shack.

She wiped a crumb from her chin.

He asked, "How did you know how to turn the boat like that?"

"I used to sail."

"Sailing, swimming, poetry. Not bad." As Nido would say, the girl was as cool as a clam on ice. "But escaping our predicament will take more information. I don't know anything about you or your family. Your father knew upper-class society, people with cabin cruisers and villas, that sort of thing. If he was a successful businessman, he belonged to financial clubs. If your mother was in society, she was probably involved with charities and good deeds. Your family must have known influential people."

"My father said you never know who your friends are until you need them."

"Well, I'm sure he had more friends than I do. We just have to reach them." He could picture her taking music lessons on a grand piano with family photographs in silver frames. "Tell me about your mother and father."

She said that her father was Vittorio Silber, the founder of a medical supply company based in Venice. He was a patriot who had served in the Great War, a generous donor to medical research and former head of the Vivaldi Musical Society. Adèle Silber, Vittorio's wife, hosted the most sophisticated parties on the Lido during opera season, and during the film festival she set up a tent on the beach. No one could believe with Vittorio Silber's connections that he would ever be threatened by Italy's new race laws. Neither parent was observant but they were both Jews. Or, to put it another way, no Jews were more assimilated into Italian society than the Silbers.

"The doctors at San Clemente took in a lot of us. Someone there must have told the SS, because when they raided the hospital they had our names. Father hid me in a laundry chute and denied I was ever with them, but the SS had a list. Then the SS marched my parents and the other Jews out of the building."

"Did you recognize any of the SS?" he asked.

"Only the officer you threw down the well."

"No uncles or aunts?"

"No. Our friends were taken with my parents. Where do you think they went? Probably just put in prison, right?"

"Probably."

"You're kind." She cleared her throat. "Anyway, do you have a family?"

He was caught off stride. "Hard to say."

"What does that mean?"

"It means that my younger brother is dead, my

father is dead, and my mother tries to run my life. That's it in a nutshell."

He hoped that was it, but she asked, "How come you're not married?"

"I am. I mean, I was. She's dead. She died in an air raid."

"In Venice?"

"In Milan."

"Do you have any children?"

"No."

"Why was she there?"

"She was on a movie set."

"Why?"

"She was an actress."

"On film?"

"Yes."

Giulia as good as sniffed. "You can hardly call that acting. I'd say 'mimicry.'"

"You know, you're just a little bit of a snob."

"When it comes to film versus the theater, yes, I guess I am," she admitted. "Do you have a photograph of her?" Cenzo let her see a studio picture and Giulia suddenly sounded very young. "I don't believe it," she said.

"She was beautiful," Cenzo said. "She was wasted in Pellestrina."

"And she got to Milan? How did anyone discover her out here?"

"It happens. Strange things happen to a woman who is truly beautiful."

"Like *Beauty and the Beast*. What was your wife's name?"

"Gina."

"How did anyone discover her? Was it a movie agent?"

"As I said, someone who happened to be in Pellestrina."

"How does anyone *happen* to visit Pellestrina?"

"Someone with family here."

"Like a brother?"

"What makes you say that?"

"You said there were three *putti di mare*. Three brothers. The younger one died, there's you, and there must have been an older brother."

"What do you mean?"

"Did your wife leave you for your older brother?" She had begun in jest but, midway, saw that she had stumbled on the truth.

"I think that's enough history for today," Cenzo said.

"What was his name?"

"Giorgio."

"Giorgio Vianello, the actor? He was one of my mother's favorites. Was he in love with your wife?"

"You make them sound like a story from a romance magazine."

"That's what it sounds like."

All of which made Cenzo the butt of the joke. "So, if I was the Beast and Gina was Beauty, what did that make Giorgio?"

"Prince Charming."

"I suppose you're right." He lit a cigarette. "Okay, it's my turn. Do you have any brothers or sisters?"

"Just me. Father made a joke out of it. He called me his 'favorite.' "

"I can see why. So, while the SS were rounding up all the Jews in the hospital, you hid in the laundry. Did they search for you?"

"Of course. I told you, they had a list of names."

"And then what did you do?"

"I worked my way down to the water and swam along the marsh."

"You're a good swimmer."

"We used to have a summer house on a lake in the mountains."

"So you swam from San Clemente."

"Until I found you."

"And pretended to be dead. That didn't show much trust."

"I don't trust anyone."

"That's wise."

The sky reverberated as a formation of Allied bombers headed up the coast. Resistance from German fighter planes had virtually disappeared, but there would be ack-ack bursting like night-blooming flowers.

She had dark edges and angles that would probably scare off the average boy. Her eyes had a forbidding quality that was unnerving, and when he thought how she recited Byron's "bubbling groan, / Without a grave," he also had to consider the possibility that she had a sense of humor.

Giulia asked, "Were you married a long time?"

"Four months. I think it was longer for her than for me. She needed more than I could give her. You can't blame her, not when she could become a movie star."

"And Giorgio helped her?"

"He had connections." That should have been explanation enough. He had started the conversation as a means of getting the girl to talk. Now the conversation had turned around. "Giorgio was a hero. When he was a boy, he was picked out of an aquacade by Mussolini himself and sent for special training. He learned to fly and to operate a one-man submarine. Once a year he would come by Pellestrina to have his picture taken and demonstrate that he had risen the common folk. He sank a British warship with a limpet mine, you know, all by himself. They made a film about it, *The Lion of Tripoli*. The movie ended in a homecoming scene with all the pretty girls in Pellestrina lined up on the dock to cheer as he landed his seaplane. Gina shouldn't have been in the shot, because she was married, but there weren't so many pretty girls in Pellestrina. Giorgio noticed her. I was myself flattered when he agreed to have dinner at our house. My mother was transported. Giorgio paid a lot of attention to Gina, but I thought that was the way movie people were. Outgoing, laughing all the time. Apparently, in the midst of that, they fell in love just like in the movies. He had the studio invite her to Turin for a screen test and a week after that I got a telegram saying she wasn't coming back. She started making one film and then she was dead."

"And?"

"I told you. A month later she was making a film with Giorgio in Milan when a bomb came through the roof."

"Were you happy?"

"Not really."

Giulia insisted, "But you must have hated her."

"No."

"You would have taken her back?"

"In an instant."

Giulia studied him. "You're crazy. When I hate, I hate for good. So, what am I supposed to do now?" She set her jaw. "Hide in the sails like a *putta di mare*?"

"If you want to."

"Maybe I do."

"Do you really want to know the truth about the *putti*—why we slept in the sails?"

"Why?"

"To avoid the cockroaches. Now you know."

7

Cenzo's mother and Celestina came after him with shawls flying like black hens running on the dock.

"Please," his mother said. "Don't make any trouble."

"Do as your mother tells you," Celestina said.

"Tells me what?"

"Nothing." His mother sniffed as they passed women tatting lace. Lacemaking, knotting and re-knotting string into intricate patterns, was an art that demanded gossip. Pellestrina was a small pond and the slightest scandal created ripples. Sofia Vianello was accustomed to being a leader of idle speculation, not its object. At least Giulia was in the shack and out of the way.

"Be good," she begged Cenzo.

"I am nothing if not good." He had only come to the dock to replace his broken oar, but his sail was an announcement that he was coming ashore. When they reached the house, his mother ushered everyone into the kitchen and sat them around the table under a row of bronze pots that hung from the beams. Whatever his mother was up to, he wished she would do it quickly.

He knew as soon as he heard footsteps on the stairs. They were highly polished footsteps,

Cenzo thought. Giorgio Vianello was a man constructed of expensive parts: an English suit, a French pomade, a signet ring that suggested a noble family, white teeth, and an Errol Flynn mustache. He had not so much lost his Pellestrina accent as traded it for one more vague and elegant. People compared him to Clark Gable. In fact, he was not much of an actor, but he was a hero and he usually played a version of himself: a submarine commander, a fighter pilot, a wounded officer in love with a beautiful nurse. Prince Charming, as Giulia had said.

"What are you doing here?" Cenzo asked.

"Visiting my family," Giorgio said.

"Now that you've visited, you can go."

Sofia Vianello put four glasses and a bottle of wine on the table. "Sit, sit. Giorgio brought this good wine. It's not every day I see both living sons."

Giorgio pulled out a chair for Celestina, who nearly swooned at the courtesy.

"I'm not going to drink with him," Cenzo said.

"Suit yourself," Giorgio said. "I'm drinking to my mother."

"Please." Sofia filled the glasses.

Cenzo would have gone, but he didn't want it said he had been chased from his own home. Besides, he wanted to gather more clothing for Giulia. Although he would not drink any of Giorgio's wine, he sat.

"So, what are you now, a general at least?"

"I'm sure he is," Sofia said. "Look at him. They say Il Duce asks his advice about everything."

"Mama, Il Duce has yet to ask my advice."

"Well, he should. Things would be going a lot better. Your brother Hugo would still be with us."

"To Hugo." Giorgio raised his glass.

Cenzo found himself forced to drink and Giorgio smiled as if he had taught a child a basic move in chess.

"So, are you a general?" Cenzo asked.

"No, I'm in the Propaganda Ministry."

"I would think that there wouldn't be much propaganda at the end of a war."

"The opposite. There is more all the time."

"Why is that?"

"It's over."

"Did we win?"

"I'm afraid not."

That was the last thing Cenzo expected to hear from his brother.

"The war is over and we lost?"

"We're down to our last few maniacs. Hitler has a new secret weapon. He *always* has a new secret weapon. He had rockets and jets but the other side has the Red Army."

"Has anyone told Il Duce?"

"The man with the short straw."

"Who is that?"

"No one will say."

"Will anything happen to you?" Celestina asked.

"No. I was just a soldier following orders and later I was merely an actor reading a script. They're not going to do anything to me."

Cenzo hoped not. He wanted the pleasure of personally strangling his brother.

"If the war is almost over, why are the Germans still rounding up Jews?"

"I told you, they're maniacs."

"The SS is raiding hospitals. It makes no sense," Cenzo said.

"What do you care?"

"Why are you here, really? It's a little late to become a fisherman."

"Do you really want to know?"

"I'm dying to hear."

Giorgio refilled the glasses. "The war is over, or as good as, and we have to look towards the future. We're going to need capable people to put Italy together again. Good, honest people untainted by the past."

"Do you know anyone like that?" Cenzo asked.

"Oh, yes. You'd be surprised."

"In Venice?" Celestina was rapt.

"Venice in particular."

"Who?"

"I'm getting ahead of myself. All I can say is that, when the dust is settled, competent people will take over, us or the Reds."

"The communists?" Sofia asked.

"I'm afraid so. We can only hope that true patriots see the opportunity and step forward."

"So now this is an opportunity," Cenzo said.

"Seen in the right light."

"You have always managed to do that." Cenzo stood. "Well, I have to go now. Should I tell everyone that you have declared the war lost?"

"I would deny it. I would never put our mother in such an embarrassing position."

"Spoken like a diplomat."

"Good to see you too," Giorgio said.

Cenzo resisted the temptation to ball his hand into a fist and hit Giorgio in the face. Perhaps Giorgio could win a fight—Prince Charming usually did—but Cenzo would have the satisfaction of forever altering Giorgio's smile. That they could have a polite conversation and never utter Gina's name was maddening, especially the way his mother was so prim a guarantor of good behavior and the way Celestina played her role as if she were in a Hollywood melodrama.

"Cenzo," Giorgio said, "I miss Gina as much as you do."

Cenzo left before he lost control. Giorgio had played his hand well. What claim did a husband have compared to the passion of a lover?

While Cenzo was gone, Giulia examined the shack. She was curious. When it came to literature or the arts he seemed virtually uneducated. But when it came to the sea, he was an encyclopedia. For her, the Lido was a playground of cabanas and amusement parks, of celebrities and socialites. The world of fishermen could have been invisible. She was beginning to realize that, for Cenzo, her world did not exist, while the lagoon teemed with life that she never had been aware of.

"Such a precocious child," had been the description that followed Giulia. "Such a handsome family." All the Silbers were admired. Silber parties were soirees where wit flowed like champagne, composers entertained at the piano and tables glittered with silver, crystal, and candlelight. Adèle Silber wore Schiaparelli and Chanel and Vittorio Silber dressed like a financier in dark, double-breasted suits. It was ridiculous to compare Cenzo to them, yet here their daughter was in clothes most suitable for fishing.

Up to the end, her father said that Italy was not another Poland or Hungary or Ukraine or France, because Italian Jews were Italians first. He was sure that Mussolini would stand up to Hitler and was humiliated when Mussolini capitulated to the Führer and began rounding up the Jews.

Like Rapunzel, Giulia whiled away the time. She opened the two wooden lockers Cenzo had warned her not to touch. Each had a hasp but no lock. Why would they? she thought. He probably had nothing to hide. Inside the first box were ordinary watercolor sketches of sunsets, seascapes, fishing boats, and, defter than she expected, a dramatically beautiful woman with dark-blond hair.

The second box had a jar of brushes, tubes of oil paint, turpentine, a metal lid used as a palette, and a painted scene of a fishing boat at sea. In the picture an American fighter plane was strafing the boat with fiery bullets. Two fishermen were drowning while another knelt on deck and prayed to a glowing vision of a Madonna. Giulia could tell the ship was the *Fatima* by the three cherubs on its sail. She studied the picture as if it chronicled a genuine miracle. The plane swooped down like the fury of God. The drowning man rolled his eyes. The Madonna watched with the equanimity of a doll.

Sailing back to the shack, Cenzo wondered who was worse, him or Giorgio? And why did he feel that he, not Giorgio, was the Prodigal Son? He tied the *Fatima* to the shack's ladder and was halfway in the door when he saw Giulia sitting cross-legged on the floor. She held shears and was surrounded by thick black clippings of hair.

"What have you done?" he asked.

She offered a smile. "I'm a fisherman."

"A what?"

"A fisherman. Nobody's going to see me, but if they do, this way they'll think I'm a boy."

"Don't be ridiculous. You know nothing about fishing."

"But I can look the part."

He walked around her. She had cropped her hair into a shaggy nightmare.

"You wouldn't fool a blind man."

"I thought it would help."

"You were wrong."

Her smile collapsed.

"Did it occur to you that's what they do to women who collaborate?" he asked. "That's what you look like, a little collaborator. How is that going to help? If you're so smart, think."

She curled up where she sat and choked back fury; he felt the constriction in his own throat. Giulia went down to the *Fatima* and Cenzo knew that if there had been any other place to go, she would have disappeared. Too late, it occurred to him that, for a proud girl, her hair was not a sacrifice lightly dismissed. A "Beast" she had called him. She was right, that's what he was. He found her sitting in the stern, her gaze fixed in the direction of Venice. Other fishing boats passed by in the dark, intent on being first to market.

"I wish my father were here," she said.

"I wish so too. He would tell you the lagoon is wider than you think."

"You're heartless. I can see why your wife left you."

He agreed. He hadn't given her a chance. Besides, constant quarreling was exhausting. It wasn't his picture of himself. He was ashamed.

"I apologize. I'm sorry for what I said about your hair."

"It was a stupid idea."

"No, it was a clever idea. I was in a foul mood and I took it out on you."

"You can keep your apologies. I don't want them."

"I was stupid."

"*Tu es encore un ingrat et un fou.*"

"That sounds right."

"As soon as it's light, I want you to leave me off," she said.

"If that's what you want."

"I never want to eat fish again in my life."

"I understand."

"You're very agreeable all of a sudden."

"The life of a fisherman is not for everyone." Cenzo leaned against the gunwales to see the stars glimmer and shine. "Do you know the constellations?"

"I studied them."

"That's good, because you'll never be lost at night if you know your constellations. That's important at sea. Stars can be guardian angels looking out for you."

"You're superstitious."

"All fishermen are superstitious. We need all the help we can get."

She hesitated. "I have a confession to make. I saw a painting in the locker you said not to look in. It was of a fisherman drowning. Was that your brother Hugo?"

"Yes."

"Did you paint that?"

"Yes."

"Then he didn't just drown, he was killed by American planes?"

"That's right."

"Do you hate them?"

He considered the question. "When you switch sides in the middle of the war, it gets very confusing."

"It's as if you have two versions of the truth?"

"Just in case."

"I was serious about leaving. I can't hide out in your shack forever."

"You could help around the boat. Everyone knows I'm short a crewman." He ran his hand over her head. Although her hair looked spiky, it was as soft as silk. "I'll introduce you to some fish."

8

Giulia insisted on a visit to San Clemente. Cenzo didn't feel he could deny her a farewell; most people got to stand by the graveside when their parents died. He stirred the water with an oar while she scanned the island through binoculars.

"But at least we should fish," Cenzo said. "If the Germans are watching, they will find it odd if we don't."

"Do you think they found the body in the well?"

"By now, yes. I'm surprised they didn't find him right away."

"I don't feel bad about killing him." She turned her face away all the same.

"You didn't kill him, I did." He let that soak in.

Cenzo had trimmed her hair to make it slightly less manic. She stared down at a school of pipefish that had taken refuge in the shadow of the boat. They scattered, chased by an eel that unwound as it went.

"Big fish eat little fish. It's a law of nature," he said.

"Mussolini promised my father that exceptions would be made for Jewish veterans."

"Il Duce made a lot of promises. As soon as he became a puppet of the Germans, all his promises were forgotten." Maybe that was more than he should have said. Her father sounded like the kind of man who never made a mistake until he did. "How long were you in the hospital?"

"Two years. I didn't go to school. I read a lot. A lot of Freud."

"Oh."

"I could probably help you with your deep-seated psychological problems or analyze your dreams."

"How would you do that?"

"We usually start with the mother."

"That I believe. Right now I'm sure a prudent man would say it's time for us to go. We don't want to attract attention."

"My mother was very stylish," Giulia said. "She was always busy. Always opened the opera season or the film festival or Carnival."

"That must have been fun for you."

"No, I was in the way. I think I embarrassed my mother," Giulia said. "She was the queen of the beach cabanas. Men vied to rub tanning lotion on her. When they turned their backs on her because she was Jewish, it almost broke her heart. She said I was homely and had chased the men away."

"Maybe she was jealous."

"No, she had taste. And furs, she loved furs and feathers. At the end she sewed her jewelry into her furs and moved like a sloth. I have to give her credit for one thing. When she said it was time to leave Italy, it was time to go. But my father was an honorable man and thought that other men were too. Mussolini gave my father his word and my father believed him."

"And then it was too late?"

"It was too late."

He pointed. "I see smoke rising from the other side of the island, and I don't think it's a dream."

Giulia refocused. "It's probably a ferry."

80

"We'll see soon enough." In fact, he had already seen enough to make the hair stand on the back of his neck.

"I don't see anything."

"You will." He looked up at his sail, which luffed indifferently. He wasn't going to get any help there.

A gunboat rounded the island. That the Germans still patrolled San Clemente could be a good sign, Cenzo thought, if it meant they were still searching the wrong place for Giulia. But because she had wanted so badly to see San Clemente, the wrong place was exactly where she was.

As part of a fleet, the gunboat might have been a miniature war machine. In the lagoon, it was colossal. Sun reflected from the ship's bridge and Cenzo couldn't identify the officers in command, although he hoped it was not the Colonel Steiner who had been with Lieutenant Hoff. Soldiers stood along the rail, uniforms fluttering from the speed of the gunboat, which could slap over the water at thirty knots. Cenzo counted ten other fishing boats on the horizon, most taking advantage of low tide to strip clams and mussels from the lines. Others were shaking fish from nets or had shut down to nap. Cenzo couldn't tell which fishing boat the Germans were headed for. The *Barking Dog* was on one side, the *Unicorn* on the other. All he could do was head toward the sun and row.

"*Merde*," Giulia hissed. "They're heading straight for us."

"Put this on." He gave her his hat.

"They'll recognize you."

"If they're looking for me, they're looking for a crew of one. We are now a crew of two. Besides, we've got them staring into the sun. We'll blind them if nothing else."

"Maybe I should swim for it."

"I wouldn't recommend it even to your Lord Byron."

Giulia glanced back. "They're still coming. I'll drown before I let them catch me."

"They won't, as long as you do what I say. When I say 'Jump,' jump. Keep your hat on and no fancy dives. We're going into sandbars. They can't follow us forever."

"They can just shoot us."

"They won't do that. They're having too much fun."

"Fun?" she asked. "Why should we help them?"

"Because they're such a sorry lot. Pull your hat down and don't look up."

Cenzo went on rowing, ignoring the gunboat as it gained on them. Ahead, the low tide exposed bands of mud and shining sun.

The gunboat throbbed and slowed and casually blocked the *Fatima*'s exit from the sandbars. Cenzo shouted, "Jump!" and encouraged her with a push. As soon as Giulia hit the water, Cenzo drove the *Fatima* aground, traded the oar for a wooden box, and jumped in after. The gunboat came to a stop directly behind them but, rather than try to escape, Cenzo pushed the *Fatima* farther into the mud.

"What are you doing?" An SS officer in a mud-spattered uniform stepped out on the deck of the gunboat. He waved a pistol airily, as if it were a baton. "I said, what are you doing?"

"Fishing," Cenzo said.

"Fishing? Italians always have it backwards. You're supposed to fish in the sea, not the land. Or maybe you were thinking of running."

"No." Cenzo strained to see whether Colonel Steiner was one of the officers on the bridge of the gunboat.

"Maybe your skinny friend there was thinking of running."

"Why? He's a good boy."

"All Italians are good until your back is turned." The officer barked an order and two soldiers jumped down from the gunboat and aimed their pistols at Cenzo and Giulia.

Maybe these particular Germans had no sense of humor, Cenzo thought. "I'm sorry," he said. "I don't speak German so well."

"I think you speak German perfectly well. Well enough."

"I'll show you," Cenzo said.

"Show me what?"

"Fishing on land."

Cenzo leapt and came down hard on his heels, kicking and gouging the sand until a shrimp with a green shell and red swimmers appeared in the pool he dug. Cenzo skipped and danced like a Cossack, capering to the beat of his feet while at the same time he ordered Giulia to fill the box. The SS officer aimed his pistol first at Cenzo, then at Giulia, and finally laughed at these crazy Italians, these crazy Italians who danced with their fish and even offered to share their catch with the soldiers, who said, "*Nein, Nein,*" holstered their pistols, and, shaking their heads, climbed back onto their gunboat, which backed out and motored toward other fishing boats. They hadn't been after the *Fatima*; they were weary men drinking the dregs of war and ready to shoot anything that caught their eye.

Giulia dropped and sat on the ground. With a fedora and mud-spattered feet she looked not so much like a *putto di mare* as a street urchin.

"We can go now." Cenzo took his hat back.

"Go where?"

"The shack, where else?"

"And spend the rest of the day hiding?" She looked out at the broad lagoon. "Teach me how to fish."

"Are you willing to get wet and stink like a fish?"

"Better than being a prisoner. But I need a rod and reel."

"Do you? I suppose if you're a rich man and have all day to catch a fish, that's one way to go about it. But if you're a professional fisherman and have to catch a thousand, you use a net. You don't chase the fish with a hook and sinker, you welcome him to your net. And you don't set your net anywhere but in a channel that is your family's birthright for generations. Do you think you can do that?"

"You said I could."

With her badly cropped hair, she put him in mind of a cat sinuously winding herself around his legs.

"Very well, we'll see."

"The goby is an ugly customer," Cenzo explained. "He's full of spines and guile and you have to get down on all fours in the water and feel around in the mud, because you can't use a rod or a net. And you have to use both hands to find his tunnel—that's right, a tunnel—to catch him. He is small and, as I said, ugly. Are you sure you want to be a fisherman?"

Giulia said nothing but she appeared resolute.

"Okay," he said. "I'll show you."

Instead of kicking the water as he had for the shrimp, he walked slowly and studied the bottom of the lagoon. At low tide, algae and sea grass shifted listlessly in the water.

"We're lucky. There's one right at your feet."

"I don't see it."

"Put some water in the pail. See the hole in the sand?"

"No."

"It's covered with a little sand."

"Then how am I supposed to see it?"

"Keep looking. You get on your knees, like so. Do you see the hole now?"

"No."

"And you reach in and tickle the goby with one hand, and up he pops into the other." There was a small explosion of sediment, and a small brown fish with elaborate spines rested in Cenzo's hand. He plopped it into the pail. "Your turn."

"To do what? I never saw anything."

"I'll give you a hint. The goby has a tunnel, which means he has two holes, a front door and a back. Knock on one door, and he comes out the other. Just be sure not to grab the spines the wrong way."

"This is stupid."

"There's a hole right here and its companion hole right there. See it?"

"Maybe."

"You have to get lower than that."

"I am."

"Lower. See the hole?"

"I see it, I see it."

"Get your hands in position."

"I'm—" A goby emerged and zipped away. "*Merde*, they're fast."

"Well, you tried."

"Wait, I think I see another hole."

"You do?"

"I have it now. Ouch! *Merde*! I lost it." She sucked blood from the tip of her finger.

"Spines."

"They're so little, why would anyone bother catching them?"

"Because if you put this ugly fish into risotto and simmer it until it disappears, you will have the most delicious dish in the world. And the market pays accordingly. Anyway, you gave fishing a try. It's not for everyone."

"I see another hole."

"You want to try again?"

"It's more interesting than sitting in the shack."

"You're soaked."

"So are you." She crept up on another hole.

"First patiently, then quickly," he said.

The goby squirted from her grasp.

"*Merde*! Almost."

"This is something else we have to talk about. Your vocabulary is all wrong. Nobody says *merde*. We're not in France. Say *merda* like an Italian, like you mean it."

"Here's another."

As a crab lifted a stalk of eelgrass, a blunt pugnacious fish peeked out. Giulia thrust her hand into the fish's hole and it darted directly into the grasp of her other hand. She transferred the fish immediately to the pail.

"I did it! I did it! I did it!"

"That's not what a fisherman says when he catches a fish."

"But I did it."

"You did."

"Things you should know: A clean boat never makes money. A red moon makes the blood boil. Never fish the same ground two days in a row. At the market, cover your old fish with your fresh. A real fisherman doesn't need boots. Fish jump to breathe. The captain of a fishing boat sleeps at the stern, the crew at the bow. Fishermen know how to wash dishes with sand. The best soup is at the bottom of the pot. When you're rowing, watch out for mines. Good luck will kiss you in bad weather."

"What about women in boats?"

"Definitely bad luck. Unless they're naked. That's good luck."

Such bad luck that Cenzo had to laugh at himself. Two days had passed since he and Giulia had fished for goby. It could be said that he had not made a real attempt to smuggle her to the mainland. How could he when she was so afraid of being left behind? But there was also the fact that she was entertaining and quick to learn.

Facts naturally landed on her shoulders. Also, he found his own miseries reduced in size when he focused on hers.

He taught her how to set a circle of nets at high tide and collect stranded fish at low. How to rake clams. How to spear a ray. How to get behind and push the boat when it ran aground. At night, watching the stars from the deck of the shack, how to track the Great Bear as he swung by his tail. How to earn the right to ask questions.

"Do you mind?" she asked.

She opened the inviolable footlocker and brought out the painting. The faint light and flicker of the lantern's flame made the picture vibrant and alive. Cenzo's brother Hugo was sinking into foamy waves, but he waved at a fighter plane that returned the favor with golden bullets. Cenzo was still on board and on his knees, praying to a vision of the Virgin that hovered in midair. The fishing boat, a larger version of the *Fatima*, was on fire. Flames climbed up the sail of the three *putti de mare.* The detail surprised Cenzo for no good reason. He was, after all, the artist. Those were his half-squashed tubes of oil paints in intense proto-colors. Greens and blues that were almost black. Cadmium red smeared like blood.

He remembered how the whites of Hugo's eyes—zinc with a hint of cerulean blue—rolled like those of a man marching to a firing squad, while the plane, a Mustang as smooth and immaculate as the Virgin, turned for a second strafing run that was louder and higher in pitch. And the Virgin blessed it. She blessed the bullets that tore Hugo apart. She blessed Celestina and her heavy sighs. She blessed Il Duce and his Black Shirts in the mountains. But she did not bless Cenzo, because he did not believe in this war and his sole intent was to outlive it.

9

For a fisherman, the subject of nets was deep and complex. A *bragotto* could be towed by two people collecting small fry, whereas a *baicolera* was a winged net designed to catch the noble sea bass. A *seragia* had as many as six nets staked in a circle. A *saltarello* was a spiral net for sea bream and shad. A half-moon net was a *mezza luna*. Most ingenious and beautiful of all was *pesca il cielo*, a net that floated high above the water to "fish the clouds."

And there were seasons. Fish left the lagoon in the wintertime and didn't return until March to lay eggs in warm water. There was fidelity; swordfish swam together, male and female. There were troublemakers: spider crabs trying to get free made a mess out of nets. Dolphins made a banquet out of fish trapped in the nets. Every net, no matter how different its design, ended in a death chamber.

Most mysterious of all creatures was the soft-shelled crab. At the first tinge of dawn, Cenzo took Giulia into a swamp where narrow channels wended through tall spartina grass. At a dock were stacks of boxes and bags and a dozen indolent cats.

"October is the best time for catching crabs, November's not so bad, and in winter they've gone out to sea. March, they're back to lay their eggs. In June you have to check the crab pots twice a day. That's your calendar."

"What if someone steals them when you aren't here?"

"That won't do thieves any good, unless they know crabs."

"A crab is a crab."

"No. The expensive delicacy that the rich devour in two bites at a fancy restaurant is a female that has just shed its shell." As Cenzo sorted through the top box, a gray crab not much larger than a bottle cap hung on to his hand by a claw. He tossed it aside and the nearest cat delicately pounced. "So, how do you know which is a female and how do you know when it's going to molt?"

"I don't know."

"You don't know because fishermen keep the

secret to themselves." He rapidly picked through other crabs in the box, reserving some in a bag and tossing the rest into the water. "First of all, you want to make sure they're good and soaked because you're selling them by the pound."

"Well?" she asked.

"Well what?"

"Aren't you going to tell me the secret?"

"I'll show you." He placed a crab in a bowl of water. "That's going to molt in two minutes."

"Neither of us has a watch."

"I'll take your word for when time is up."

"It doesn't matter. It's not doing anything."

"Just wait." He picked through the boxes while she examined the crab in the bowl from every angle.

"Just wait?"

"Like I said."

" 'Such hath it been—shall be—beneath the sun / The many still must labor for the one!' Byron."

"I expected nothing less. Is there, by any chance, anyone else you like?"

"*King Kong* was a favorite of mine."

"The strong and silent type."

"For years we barely left the house. We had a projector and watched the same films over and over. We must have watched *King Kong* ten times. It was a real Beauty and the Beast story."

"Why do I have the feeling this is not going to be flattering?"

"What I mean is that it's a real love story. In fact, it may be the truest love story of all."

"You saw *King Kong* too many times."

"In fact, it's just like Dante. About thirty seconds to go. In *The Divine Comedy*, the poet Dante falls in love with Beatrice the same way the giant gorilla, Kong, falls for Fay Wray. I don't know why they call it a comedy. Laurel and Hardy are a comedy."

She gave a start as the back of the crab's shell split and the crab began to crawl backwards out of itself, out of its shield and claws, nibbling at odd pieces like a tenant leaving a tidy home.

On the way back, Cenzo lowered the sail and punted through a maze of grass islands and channels so narrow and shallow that at times he had to lift the rudder to ease the *Fatima* through. An egret measured the channel in self-absorbed steps while swallows darted in and out of the mist. Broken duck blinds stood along a pond.

Giulia said, "In the wintertime, my father and his friends used to shoot ducks. I remember him coming home with bloody birds and saying he had 'bagged the limit.'"

Cenzo had guided hunters into the marsh during duck season. He remembered the rich men with their oiled boots, flasks of whiskey, and expensive guns. He also remembered having to dive for cover when one of the guests took a shot. Of course, there had been no hunting since the war began.

Giulia was off in a new direction. "Do you like your brother's movies?"

"I'm not a film critic."

He had seen only one of his brother's films. *The Lion of Tripoli* had been screened with much fanfare at the Palace of Cinema on the Lido. The family had been given a place of honor, and Gina stifled her alarm over the perils the celluloid Giorgio faced with a handkerchief he gave her.

"It's hard to believe you're the brother of Giorgio Vianello."

"I couldn't agree more."

She reached up and shook the lower branches of a tamarisk tree until they were enveloped by a shower of pink blossoms. The more he asked her to stop, the more branches she shook. He was not in a mood to play games. At the same time, it was a relief to see her enjoy the moment like a child and throw blossoms into the air.

"I wish we didn't have to leave," Giulia said absentmindedly.

"I know." For a moment he stood still, if only for a rest. She stiffened and he asked, "What's the matter?"

Giulia pointed ahead where the blossoms were overhung with shadow. "There's another boat."

The *Fatima* glided up to a boat as narrow as a punt and nudged it. The boat was empty. That was his first concern. Then they took in its peculiarities: the fact that it was barely wide enough for a man to lie down in, that it was built as low to the waterline as a crocodile, and that a musket almost as large as a cannon protruded from the bow.

"What is it?"

"It's a duck gun," Cenzo said. "A *s'ciópon*."

"Not like my father's."

"No, it wouldn't be."

The *s'ciópon* was a single-barrel shotgun mounted directly on a boat and designed to blow a hole in a flock of birds. It was not a subtle weapon. It sounded like a cannon and could bring down fifty or more ducks with one shot.

The boat lay in a bower of cobwebs that winked in the sunlight. Water pooled in the hollow carved for a hunter to lie in. Ropes tied the gun to stakes fore and aft with slack enough to allow for the rise and fall of tides, but not enough for the gun to wander away.

"How long do you think it's been here?" Giulia asked.

"Two months, at least." He lifted the lid of the firing chamber and extracted a moldy oversized shotgun cartridge.

"Would it work?"

"It's a little like using a hammer to kill a fly, but if you cleaned and oiled the gun, it should work. It's a death trap."

She watched him toss the cartridge aside.

"I've got more of these at the shack," Cenzo said.

"It gives me goose bumps."

"Well, it's a nasty piece of work."

A discolored rope connected the trigger to a trip wire at the end of the barrel. The gun was a trap that had never been sprung. It had been meant for somebody, though. Someone had been expected to stand where Cenzo stood and be cut down. Anyway, the girl had not noticed and it was nothing she needed to know about.

It was dark by the time Cenzo delivered the crabs and returned to the fishing shack. Giulia had set out a dinner of sausage and cheese. She had become a different person from the girl he had found floating in the lagoon. She pulled more than her weight on deck. Her jibes were fewer and she acted inter-ested in the art of fishing. He didn't believe it for a moment, but it was a nice effort on her part.

"Maybe I'll get you a rod and reel after all so you can battle the mighty sea bass. Then you will have a struggle on your hands."

"What else would be fun?"

"Octopus is an interesting character. He wiks at you and disappears. Squid is a torpedo. Flatfish are clowns with two eyes on one side because God has a sense of humor. And a cuttlefish is not so much a fish as an inverted mollusk that swims backwards."

"What—"

Cenzo abruptly put a finger to his lips and pointed below the shack. He turned the lamp to its dimmest flame and motioned Giulia to lie in the darkest corner. He slipped a gutting knife into his hand.

A massive but familiar figure rose from the ladder.

"Nido."

"The same." The bartender hauled himself up through the floor of the shack and into a more comfortable position.

Cenzo tossed the knife aside. "Don't you ever knock?"

"You have so many visitors?" Nido was in a ratty sweater and a beret reminiscent of his days in Paris as a boxer. "This place is as dark as a coal mine. Do you mind?" Nido turned up the lamp's flame. "Having a little repast, are we? A picnic for two?" He looked significantly at the corner where Giulia curled up. "I wasn't invited?"

"I'm taking care of a nephew from Milan. His parents thought he would be safer here."

"Than Milan?"

"Than Milan."

"An odd choice." Nido picked at a scrap of ham. "What's his name?"

"Marco."

"He's helpful?"

"He shows promise."

"High praise coming from you. You must be working him like the devil. Look at the boy. Sound asleep."

"Don't wake him."

"Well, I just wanted to come by and see how you were. You should bring little Marco around the bar to say hello."

"I may do that."

"All that rowing makes a man thirsty," Nido said. Cenzo poured out two glasses of grappa that Nido sniffed.

"Swill," he said.

"You sold it to me."

"So I should know."

"Another?"

"Why not?" Nido picked at the ham and bread. "Cenzo, I thought we had an understanding that we wanted no part in this war. We were going to be bystanders."

"What makes you think I'm not?"

"Nobody's seen you for days."

"So?"

"People have noticed how you steer clear of other boats. How you suddenly have someone else on deck. How you no longer come to the bar, even to catch Farina's Fascist dick in the doorjamb."

"What's your point?"

"My point, dear friend, is that you and I have made a commitment to stay out of this idiotic war. Now, I'm not so sure about you. The

Germans have come by asking about you. That's always a bad sign, won't you agree?"

"Asking what?"

"General questions. One question in particular: Are you a Jew?"

"That's ridiculous. Vianellos have been here forever."

"That's what I told them."

Giulia sat up cool and collected. "He's not a Jew. He's the brother of Giorgio Vianello, the movie star."

"Ah, this is, I take it, your 'nephew.' My God. And unless I have completely lost my eyesight and my wits, 'he' is a 'she.' "

"So now you know," Cenzo said.

"This is, you understand, a deception that won't last a minute in daylight."

"We've done pretty well so far."

"Well, dear boy, the Germans smell something. They found the body of an SS officer down a well. Do you know anything about that?"

"No," Cenzo said.

"It was self-defense," said Giulia.

Nido rubbed his face. "Cenzo, how could you get into so much trouble in the middle of a fucking lagoon?"

"I just have to get the girl somewhere safe. I've smuggled things on the black market before."

"You smuggled cigarettes. This is different. Ask your friend Russo: the Gestapo arrested him."

Giulia got to her feet. "I can hide someplace else. My father said the war will be over in a matter of weeks."

"And where is your father now?" Nido asked. "The SS are in some kind of final frenzy. They're more dangerous than ever."

"Then I can go on my own."

Cenzo said, "Do you hear that, Nido? A girl is willing to go where grown men are afraid to tread. How does that make you feel?"

"That *my* skin comes first. Fortunately for you, I am the only one in Pellestrina who has connected the arrival of your 'nephew' to the escape of a Jewish girl."

"Giulia. Her name is Giulia."

"It's not like you to pull a stunt like this, Cenzo, not like you at all." Nido turned his attention to Giulia. "How old are you?"

"Eighteen."

"She's just a kid," Cenzo said.

"Eighteen is not a kid," Nido said. "Open your eyes."

"We're talking about hiding here for a few more days, a week at the most," Cenzo said. "You know everyone in Pellestrina. Can you put me in touch with partisans?"

"Which band of partisans? The communists? Socialists? Anarchists? They'd as soon shoot at each other as at a stranger. Usually I would say drop her off with a sympathetic family, a nun or a priest, but not with Squadron Leader Farina nosing around."

"So?"

"So that's your answer." He heaved himself to his feet. "Come to the bar tomorrow. Alone, just yourself. In the meantime, all I can tell you is what I told Primo Carnera: 'Stay down!' "

IO

Cenzo was sailing to Pellestrina from the shack when he was surprised by the sound of an airplane. It did not have the symphonic drone of a multi-engine bomber or the intense buzz of a fighter plane.

Instead it reminded him of the small aircraft that used to tow banners over the Lido before the war: "Hotel Excelsior" or "Cinzano." It took daring to fly one and challenge enemy domination of the sky. The pilot deliberately drew a crowd by flying nearly low enough to touch the rooftops. Lower until it flashed across windowpanes, sails, and nets hung to dry. Lower still until it touched down on pontoons, skied over water, and feathered to a stop by the village promenade.

The plane was a two-seater Stork designed for wartime reconnaissance—but planes rarely visited Pellestrina, let alone in the middle of the war. The pilot opened a door, stepped out onto a pontoon, and waved to spectators who gathered. When he was recognized, a cheer went up. He was a movie star, the "Lion of Tripoli." He was Giorgio Vianello in tweeds, with aviator goggles hung jauntily around his neck and a Hollywood smile for the crowd.

Giorgio took Pellestrina's one and only motorboat to the dock. By the time Cenzo tied up the *Fatima* his brother was ambling along the houses that faced the dock, accompanied by a photographer and an entourage of children who marched like soldiers. On the fringe was a pudgy Farina Junior, the Son of the She-Wolf, in his black Fascist short pants and carrying his wooden rifle. Women who were tatting lace in the alleyways went still, needles poised, and surreptitiously tracked Giorgio's progress with their eyes. This was, after all, the leading man of *We March on Rome*, *The Young Marconi*, and *The Lion of Tripoli*. His flesh had pressed against the flesh of famous actresses, and if he had transgressed, it only made him more romantic and, perhaps, irresistible. That he had fallen in love with a married woman like Gina Vianello only stamped him as a man of passion.

As he passed a market, a greengrocer rushed out to press an apple into his hand. The photographer, a hawk-eyed man in a straw hat, stepped forward with a flash camera to memorialize the moment.

Cenzo had been on his way to Nido's, but

Giorgio's entourage exerted a gravitational pull of curiosity that was irresistible, and he trailed behind.

At a bicycle repair shop, Giorgio approved a poster of a boy donating his tire to a soldier on a motorcycle under the question: "Rubber? Who Needs It More?" At a window box thick with geraniums he presented a "Certificate of Fascist Sacrifice" to a mother who had lost her sons in combat. At a sweetshop he bought lollipops for all the children and, after posing for more photographs, sent them on their way. The crowd dwindled down to Cenzo.

"Want me to stay?" the photographer asked Giorgio.

"No, it's just my brother."

The photographer looked Cenzo up and down and found his statement humorous. He bummed a cigarette from Giorgio and sauntered back toward the center of town.

"What is this circus all about?" Cenzo asked. "Happy times on the home front?"

"It gets me away from the radio station."

"At the cost of possibly being shot down."

"Would you like it if I had been shot down?"

"Yes."

"It's better than the General Staff's back-stabbing and boredom." Giorgio lit cigarettes from a silver lighter for himself and Cenzo. It had a willow pattern that he held out for Cenzo to admire. "Japanese. The detail is amazing. And if you touch a hidden spring . . ." The bottom opened to reveal a short barrel and a 22mm round. "A gift from the Japanese envoy. A fascinating people, the Japanese. But doomed."

"No more than us."

"Much more. Italians adjust. You don't find Japanese changing sides in the middle of a war."

Giorgio tried to hand the lighter to Cenzo. "A gift."

"No, thank you."

"I insist." Giorgio handed the lighter to Cenzo.

"No."

"You never change. It's been ten months since she left you, eight months since she died. Time to move on." Giorgio returned the case to his jacket. "I hear you're not happy about marrying Celestina. Most men would be overjoyed to have a woman like her. She's pretty enough, in a bouncy fashion. Why not make your mother happy?"

"You mean make *you* happy? Salve your conscience?"

Giorgio laughed. "You're wasted as a fisherman. You should have been a priest."

"What makes you so sure I'm not going to kill you?"

"You would have by now, but I have to admit that the prospect keeps me on my toes."

"Go fuck yourself."

"I have news about your friend Russo. Is Nido's bar open?"

It was where Cenzo was headed anyway.

This early, they had the bar to themselves. Nido brought glasses of Campari. "I trust if you're going to shoot each other, you'll do it outside." He retreated behind the bar, where he made himself busy wiping glasses.

Giorgio settled into a booth. "Nothing has changed. It has authentic Venetian charm. Your seashell mural and Nido's boxing pictures. Do they still serve clams and spaghetti here?"

"No. The cook was killed at Anzio."

"That's a shame. *Cin Cin!*"

"To the pointlessly dead." Cenzo touched glasses. "The cook is dead, Giovanni who used to play the accordion and Scarpa Junior the shoemaker are dead, a dozen fishermen you grew up with are dead, killed on this beach or in that lemon grove because of the war. A war you promote. Just as you're selling it today. You were a hero, now you're a salesman."

"Well, it's almost over." Giorgio leaned back.

"So you said."

"Does Nido still tell those outlandish boxing stories?"

"Ask him yourself."

Giorgio was not so inclined. He waved away cigarette smoke. "Do you have any idea how small the world is?" Giorgio asked.

"The lagoon seems fairly large."

"Perhaps. Imagine how different perspectives can be to a horse, to a crab, to a dove. Really, Cenzo, sometimes you drive me crazy. Remember how I used to do your homework?"

"I didn't like school."

"Too bad, I guess you'll always be a fisherman. You might have gotten an education."

"Your kind of education. I remember how you won a prize in school for your Fascist essays. Total horseshit. Why aren't you in Salò ironing Mussolini's pants?"

"Salò is full of diehards who are willing to do that."

"Even now?"

"Even now."

"What about the Germans?" Cenzo asked.

"The Germans live in another dimension. They half exist for us and we half exist for them."

The brothers sat back and allowed Nido to pour another round.

"How's the smuggling going, Nido?" Giorgio asked.

"Without fuel for my motorboat, I've become a very honest man."

"And the boxing?" Giorgio asked.

"No more boxing," Nido said. "Cenzo can tell you: we're both pacifists."

"Both of you? That will come as a surprise to some people, I'm sure. Leave the bottle."

106

"I have some fishing to do," Cenzo said.

"Nonsense. How often do we get together for a civilized conversation?" Giorgio's photographer slipped in the door and occupied a booth. He shook off Nido's attention and put his camera on the table in front of him. He added a pistol. So maybe he was more than a photographer, Cenzo thought.

"Are you still painting miracles?" Giorgio asked. "Or did you run out of paint?"

"Ran out of miracles."

"That's too bad, I sincerely thought you had talent."

"You were going to tell me about Russo. Tell me."

"I heard he was taken in for questioning by the Germans. Is that true?" Giorgio asked.

"I don't know. There are a lot of Italians named Russo and lately there seem to be a lot of Germans," Cenzo said.

"This Russo was a fish vendor. He was detained for trading on the black market, which is a petty crime. True, everyone trades on the black market if they want to eat. But this Russo is also a communist."

"Also a lot of them, I hear."

"This one served with you in Africa. Anyway, he's been released. I thought you would like to know, in case he was a friend. Apparently, your name was mentioned. Do you know why?"

"No."

107

"No idea?"

"None."

"Good. Then I will tell the SS there's no reason for them to bother you."

"They'll take your word for it?"

"Why not? The Germans and I have been comrades in arms for years. I ought to have a certain amount of influence. Bottoms up."

That was typical, Cenzo thought. For his brother, everything was geometry. One angle determined another angle, which determined a third angle, and so on. Giorgio would know that a Jewish girl was on the run from the hospital at San Clemente. That the *Fatima* had been intercepted in the area of the girl's escape. That Cenzo had sought out a black-market operator named Russo.

"What is your title now?" Cenzo asked.

"It changes from one day to the next. I was with the Air Ministry but the Germans won't give us any more planes or parachutes. So now I do radio broadcasts."

"A salesman of death."

"That's a little harsh. I'm one of the men trying to keep Italy together."

"How?"

Giorgio took a deep breath. "You know, it's time for me to get back to Salò. I just wanted to assure you about your friend Russo and maybe I said too much. It's been good, though, don't you think, the two of us talking like this?"

"If you say so."

Giorgio got to his feet. He started to offer his hand but thought better of it. "We should do this again."

At the door, Giorgio gathered his photographer, who, on his way out, gave Cenzo an appraisal full of suspicion.

Nido returned to the booth. "What was that about?"

"Russo is out of prison."

"Did your brother ask about the girl?"

"No, but for all I know that's what the entire meeting was about."

Giorgio didn't care about Jews one way or the other, Cenzo thought. But this late in the game, what besides Jews did the SS have to trade? Besides, the SS were the past. Cenzo had the distinct impression that Giorgio saw himself as a man of the future.

"As for the girl," Nido said, "it's my opinion that she has nothing to fear as long as she is content to stay quietly in your fishing hut. She could stay there for a year without being caught, as long as she exercises self-control."

"Content to live in a wooden box?"

"You're living in a fishing shack with her. I hope you exercise self-control."

"You sound like my mother."

Nido crossed himself. "God forbid your mother got wind of this. The very thought makes me sweat. Forget I ever brought it up."

"Done."

"Okay. As for contacts, you know how it is. All types come into the bar and you think you know who is what, but if you approach someone you think is a partisan and guess wrong, you'll be put against a wall and shot. If they are partisan and they think you're trying to infiltrate them, you'll be marched to a tree and shot. Either way, it's not good for business."

"You don't trust anyone?"

"I'm not even sure about me." Nido pushed a shiny key across the table. "For the storeroom behind the bar, as long as she doesn't mind me barging in every so often for a bottle of gin."

"Thank you."

"Take it, take it."

Cenzo tucked the key into his pocket. "I'll remember this. Something else: if Russo comes by, can you tell him I'll be fishing in the sky tomorrow?"

"What does that mean?"

"He'll know," Cenzo said.

Nido wagged his finger. "This does not mean that I'm getting involved in this moronic war. I'm simply helping a friend who has fucked up on a colossal scale. Besides, I don't trust your brother. I don't believe his sudden concern for you."

"You don't believe in brotherly love?"

"Not in this case. Let me tell you something."

"Is it another boxing story?"

"Wait. I just want to tell you this. I once boxed in Burma. I had a friend there who was a veterinarian and he had a friend, a woman, who got a pet python when it was just a baby. S'true. A beautiful snake with amber eyes. As it grew, it would coil up in her lap when she was reading and coil next to her in bed when she was asleep. One night, the veterinarian got a phone call from the woman. She was nervous because, instead of coiling, the python was stretched out next to her in bed. Completely stretched. From head to tail. The veterinarian told her to get out of bed and out of the house. He said, 'It's measuring you.'"

"What are you trying to tell me?"

"Be careful who you embrace."

Besides a murmur or two when Cenzo tied up to the hut, Giulia slept through his return. Her face was pale and delicate, her brow shining in the moonlight. Had she turned beautiful? Not in any ordinary way; more as if after days on the water she had developed the tautness of a wild animal.

For Giulia it was an unconscious pose. Cenzo lit the lantern and set its flame down to a soft arc, then opened his footlocker and brought out his sketch pad and colored pencils. Perhaps because he had to fill in what he could not see, he drew with more than the usual speed and abandon, using blue for shadow and Indian red for the outline of her cheek, letting her portrait emerge from the paper in one go before she awoke. Then drew her eyes as if they were open and looking at him.

II

High on bamboo poles was the net, "*pesca da cielo*." Set out on the edge of the swamp, it resembled nothing so much as a cloud hoisted high into the air, billowing and dripping water, accumulating all species of catch. When Cenzo tugged on a central knot, the net opened and fish rained down onto the deck of the *Fatima* as Giulia dodged out of the way.

"I'm never going to fish with you again," she said. "You're a monster."

"First I'm a beast, then a monster. Next a sea serpent?"

"Not a bad idea. You two couldn't make more noise." Eusebio Russo took shape in the mist. He was a big man with a red beard, a corduroy jacket, a rumpled hat, and one eye purple and swollen shut. He looked at Giulia. "And what sort of odd fish is this?"

"My name is Giulia."

"A girl."

"My crew," said Cenzo.

"Really? Since when do you sail with girls?"

112

"One girl," Cenzo said.

"When it comes to bad luck, one girl will do as well as a dozen. I heard her chattering a hundred meters away. Is she always so loud?"

"Quiet as a mouse and she's sober, which is more than I can say for some."

"I used to fly with him, Giulia. Did he tell you about Africa?"

"No, he didn't."

"He's too modest. When we were mere boys, he used to take photographs of us dropping poison gas on the natives. The brass didn't like that, coming from the brother of the Lion of Tripoli. So they took away our camera and our plane and shipped us home unfit for duty."

"At least it saved us from fighting for Il Duce." Cenzo checked Russo's eye. "What happened?"

"I had a run-in with the SS. I have to admit, I thought it was my funeral. I was at the opera house when they pulled me in. They meant business. Handcuffs. A bag over the head. Then, after only one punch in the eye, I was back on the street."

"You didn't notice any SS officer in particular?"

"No."

"No colonel with a scar down the side of his face that makes him look like he's been put through a meat grinder?"

"No. It all seemed to be a big mistake. Do you have a cigarette?"

Cenzo lit two Junos and handed one to Russo.

The cigarettes smoldered like damp fuses. Giulia stood still, exercising patience.

"Why were you asking for me at the fish market?" Russo asked.

"Can you get somebody to the partisans?" Cenzo asked.

Russo looked in every possible direction before asking, "This is a theoretical question?"

"Theoretical."

Russo took a deep breath. "Okay, to begin with, which partisans? Sometimes they help each other, sometimes they shoot each other. The northern region is generally controlled by the Garibaldi Brigade."

"Reds?"

"That's right. There's the church, but that's riddled with collaborators. The Holy Father kept his eyes closed for a long time."

"What about the Americans?" Giulia asked. "They're real soldiers."

"The Americans are my favorite fairy tale. 'Once upon a time, the American army took a magic sleeping powder. The end.' They should have been here a year ago. Is this why you're here in the middle of the lagoon?"

"I'm learning to fish," Giulia said.

"From my friend Cenzo? I could sell tickets to that. What are you two not telling me?"

"It's simple," Cenzo said.

"Now I'm getting nervous."

"Do you remember a German raid on the hospital on San Clemente Island two weeks ago?"

"Yes, I heard. The SS rounded up all the Jews."

"All but a girl who swam away."

"Is that so?" Russo tentatively looked at Giulia. "You're not serious."

"She's an excellent swimmer."

"Her family?"

"They were caught."

"I'm sorry, but why not just wait?" Russo said. "The German army is going to retreat sooner or later. They're not going to care about one girl who managed to escape."

"What's strange is that they are still after her. The Germans were asking about her the other day at Nido's. It's as if catching Giulia is one of the last things they want to do before they return to the Fatherland."

"It doesn't add up," Russo said. "Cenzo, my dear friend, what are you not telling me?"

"I killed an SS officer."

"See, not so simple."

"Cenzo didn't mean to," Giulia said.

"I had no choice. Hoff was trying to kill her."

"You knew the officer by name? This is rich." Russo turned to Giulia. "And you've been fishing ever since? Do you like to fish?"

"It's okay."

"But with Cenzo it has to be a passion. Everything perfect. If he says you can fish, you must be a fast learner."

"Can you help her or not?" Cenzo asked.

"Remind me, how did you find her?"

"Floating in the water."

"Like the baby Moses?"

"Like Moses."

"What is her family name?"

"Silber."

"Wealthy?"

"Yes."

"That's good, but why were they still in Venice?"

"A failure in judgment."

"And you'll vouch for all this? Because, old friend, if something goes wrong, you will be held responsible."

"Absolutely."

"Really wealthy?"

"Loaded. I'm sure she'll be generous. But you understand, she won't be able to pay you until the war is over." Cenzo could almost see Russo calculating the size of his reward.

"Very well, then I will personally escort her to a safe place."

"To Venice or the mainland?"

"Leave that to me."

"But I should come, too, at least until she's handed off."

"No. The fewer people the better. I'll come back later and tell you how it went."

"So you'll be there?"

"Cenzo, you have to stop asking questions. The Garibaldi Brigade runs its own show. No outsiders."

"They're communists?"

"Do you have any objections?"

"No."

"When can she be ready?" Russo asked.

"In a couple of days."

"Tomorrow," Russo said.

Cenzo was surprised. "Don't you need more time to prepare?"

"Why? The sooner the better, I assume."

"Where should we meet?" Cenzo asked.

"Your fishing shack will do."

Cenzo did not like being rushed. He asked, "Giulia, is this okay with you?"

She was stunned. Arms empty, she stared down at the fish that covered the deck of the *Fatima*, sardines blue as glass, bream as bright as nickel, and rays as black as ink, committing them all to memory.

As they sailed back to Pellestrina, Giulia leaned against the gunwale. Where Russo would take her, Cenzo had no idea; but for her own sake, the sooner she went the better. Still, he wasn't happy.

"Why are you getting rid of me?" Giulia asked. "I'm already a target and staying away from you isn't going to help."

"I'm simply facing reality. You need a better place to hide."

"I'm not a help?"

"You're a good help, but you shouldn't be living with me. You're not a girl anymore."

"Attractive? Unattractive?"

"Beautiful."

That stunned her into momentary silence. "What's wrong with that?" she asked.

"Just about everything."

"You think we're so different?"

"I can't think of any two people more different."

"You think I'm too young?"

"Aren't you?"

"I think you're afraid of women."

"I'm sure you're right."

"So, again, why am I a problem?"

"Do I have to spell it out for you?"

"Yes."

Cenzo slipped his hand around her waist and kissed her. He expected her to push him away, but she held the kiss like a long drink of water. He felt the heat of her face, the press of her body, and the way her leg overlapped and coiled on his.

Then he heard the rhythmic thud of the German gunboat as it approached, and he moved quickly to steer the *Fatima* out of the searchlight's range.

12

Cenzo and Giulia played a desultory game of cards while they waited in the fishing shack for Russo. Aces were tops, except for sevens, and three sevens beat everything. Neither Cenzo nor the girl had their heart in the game, though, and the cards lay forgotten on the table. Not that Cenzo thought it was likely Russo would return for her so soon, but she should be ready to leave.

"I'd feel better if you were coming," she said.

"You'll be fine."

He had argued Giulia into going. For the first time, however, it struck Cenzo that he would be passing her to men he knew nothing about. He trusted Russo, but after him came a line of shadowy figures. Italy was awash with girls bought and sold, lost and never seen again. And what would her fate be if the SS found her first?

She asked, "Do you think I'll see you after the war?"

The same question had occurred to him. Who knew what sort of place Italy would be when the Germans left? Would there be a civil war? Would Italy turn into another Russia or another America?

"I'm sure."

"But do you really think so?" She took his hand.

"I said yes. There's nothing to worry about."

"How will I find you?"

"I'm always here. I was a fisherman yesterday, I am today, and I will be one tomorrow. I'm not going anywhere."

"Innocenzo? That's your name?" She put her hand over her mouth to stifle a laugh.

Cenzo smiled but he had to ask again, "Is there anything more you can tell me about the man who betrayed you?"

In a small voice Giulia said, "I don't know who he was, but I know what he was like."

"Like what?"

"There were fifteen of us in a ward to ourselves: my father, my mother, and I, the Diaz and Columbo families, Dr. Razza the psychiatrist, DaCosta the lawyer, a banker named Blanco, and Rabbi Willenberg. We tried not to make much noise. Sometimes my father would put on a stethoscope and wander the hospital like a doctor and meet with other conspirators."

"Do you know any of their names?" Cenzo asked.

"Only my father knew. They were rounded up too. You have to understand, he had a way of making us all believe that somehow he was in charge and we would be liberated any minute. It became a normal way of life. That day, my father and the rabbi were arguing in whispers about whether they could pray without ten men to form a quorum. My father didn't really care, he just loved to argue. I had gone to the bathroom with a book to read. Well, it was sort of a bathroom. We used a basin we emptied twice a day. The book was *Gone with the Wind*. My parents were scandalized. We had been warned not to put any lights on, but I thought a candle would be allowed. Suddenly the bathroom door burst open. My father blew out the candle and said, 'They're coming,' and I heard boots and dogs on the stairs and fists pounding on the door. The attic had windows hardly big enough for a cat to pass through, so my father pushed me into a laundry chute. I clung there while Lieutenant Hoff called out the names."

"Where did he get the names?"

"From DaCosta, the lawyer. I know it was him. You know why? DaCosta was the only name never called."

"I doubt very much that DaCosta is his name now. Today, everybody has at least two names. Do you think you could identify him?"

"I can't describe him, but I know I would recognize him."

"Could anyone else in the group have escaped?"

"Everyone was taken away. They're all gone." It was the closest that Giulia had come to admitting that her father and mother were dead. "If, during a war, innocent people are taken away and killed, isn't that a crime?"

"That's a war crime, yes, and he knows who you are. That's why we have to be careful."

"But if he was guilty, wouldn't he want to hide?"

"He doesn't have to hide from the dead. It must have been quite a shock for him to discover that you escaped. Your father's advice for you to work your way to the American army might be a good idea. In fact, if you speak English, it might be smart to pretend to be American, at least at the start, so you're not just thrown into the crab pot."

"What crab pot?"

"Us. We are the crabs, climbing over each other and shedding our own shells, Fascists one moment, Reds the next."

Cenzo heard the sound of oars in the water. He looked out and saw two figures in dark clothes and dark scarves approach the shack. The lead rower lifted his scarf just long enough to show he was Russo. They didn't tie up, only motioned for Giulia to come down.

"Wait," Cenzo said. "I'm coming too."

"No. That's not the agreement," Russo said. "Hurry up. The gunboat is on patrol."

"Wait, I want to say good-bye," Giulia said.

"There's no time," Russo said.

"We're both coming," Cenzo said.

Russo said, "The people at the other end are definite. It's just the girl or no one."

"It's okay," Giulia said to Cenzo.

The boat shifted from side to side as she got in. Cenzo had not anticipated such a rush. He didn't have much of a leave-taking in mind. Nothing sentimental. But . . . something.

Russo pushed off.

They rowed standing, fore and aft, with Giulia sitting in the middle. They paused only to hand her a black scarf that rendered her invisible. And as suddenly as that, she disappeared.

13

Cenzo stood on the roof of his mother's house and helped her fold laundry while he watched the lagoon for any sign of Russo. Ten days had passed without any news of Giulia. She seemed to have flitted in and out of his life like a sprite.

Celestina, by comparison, was large and heavy, full of sighs and anxiety about being violated by American soldiers, a theme that Fascist propagandists pressed mercilessly through posters of lecherous Americans with virginal Italian women. Squadron Leader Farina had posted them on every public building.

Cenzo took his catch to the fish market and lingered to talk to Russo, but no one had seen him since the day he had disappeared with Giulia.

Nido didn't mention Giulia. "A wise man," he liked to say, "keeps his ignorance to himself." When the German gunboat patrolled the lagoon, it would flash its searchlight in the direction of

Cenzo's cabin and cruise by. Although the German army should have collapsed, it fought all the more bitterly fending off a day of judgment.

As time went on, the very atmosphere of Pellestrina changed. Germans no longer paid for the chickens they seized. Women hid their husbands in haylofts and cellars rather than allow them to be snatched off the street and trucked to German factories. Boys with wooden rifles chose to be partisans rather than Sons of the She-Wolf.

The closer the battle line drew, the more intense Celestina's attentions to Cenzo became, squeezing past him on the stairs, embellishing his package of food with smoked ham and pastries.

"You'll see," his mother said. "You've got a real treasure in that girl. She didn't deserve to have her husband die in such a terrible storm."

"It wasn't the storm that did Hugo in, it was an American fighter plane. I was there."

"And almost drowned, too, that's why you don't remember. It's too bad that Giorgio couldn't save him."

"We were short of heroes that day." It was true, he thought, little things made such a difference. Take a cowboy from Texas, teach him how to fly, send him to Italy, and make him a little unhappy about a letter from his girlfriend saying she has found somebody else. He sees this little fishing boat bobbing in the water between Venice and the Lido. He swoops down for one blast of his machine guns to relieve his pent-up anger and it feels so good that he swoops down again and again, diving into the chatter of his guns. Hugo died and, hearing the news, his father suffered a stroke and died too. So, if his mother was a little crazy, Cenzo understood.

As they finished folding the last sheet, a familiar Stork reconnaissance plane approached low over the water, touched down nose up, and taxied to the dock.

"Giorgio's here," Cenzo said.

"Back and forth, back and forth," she said, "always asking about you. See, your older brother only wants what's good for you. You always think the worst. For once, be friendly."

This time when Giorgio set down at Pellestrina and tied up to the dock, there was no rush to welcome him. Women concentrated on their lace. Mothers kept their children inside. The greengrocer and sweetshop clerk kept their samples to themselves and retreated to the shadow of their awnings. Giorgio trudged to Nido's bar and found Cenzo at the booth under the mural of the lagoon.

"I saw your plane come in. Visiting the family?" Cenzo asked.

"Visiting you. Do you mind?" Giorgio sat.

"Do you care?" asked Cenzo.

Nido stayed behind the counter and wiped glasses. The only other customers on a warm midday were the ancient Albano brothers, Enrico and Salvatore, playing cards under a trellis in the back of the bar. They maintained a steady stream of toothless threats aimed at each other.

"You were expecting me," Giorgio said.

"I heard your plane. Who else would be flying here?"

"Shouldn't I get some credit for visiting the family?"

"I don't know. You're like a snake: there's no end to you. If I see you once, I'm bound to see you again. Nido! Do you remember your story about the snake? Tell it to my brother."

"That's all right," Giorgio said. "I get the gist."

"Nido! Two grappas," Cenzo called. "We may have something to celebrate soon, like the return of our German friends to the Fatherland."

"That would call for prosecco," Nido said. "And we don't have any."

"No? Too bad. Maybe we'll just have to declare a national holiday."

"You're enjoying yourself," Giorgio said.

"To a degree."

"That's good. You are usually such an angry individual." Giorgio opened his cigarette lighter and Cenzo eased out of its secret line of fire. "I feel sorry for poor Celestina having to cope with all that anger when you get married. You are going to be married, aren't you, as soon as the war is over? Let's drink to that."

Cenzo acquiesced. How could he say no? He

was momentarily distracted by a tremor in the air, the sound of the gunboat drawing up to the dock, and the feeling of a trap shutting.

"Cheers!" Giorgio raised a glass. He didn't look like a man on the losing side of a war. If anything, he looked like Errol Flynn about to step on a soundstage to woo a leading lady. Aviation fuel was a precious commodity, and here he was, flying around the lagoon in his little two-seater airplane as if it were his personal plaything.

"Where is your photographer?" Cenzo asked. "I thought you never traveled without one."

"Maximo hates to fly. He's Sicilian. They don't trust any form of transport but the burro."

"You look dressed for a day of shooting grouse."

"Whereas you smell like fish. To each his own. I think that's what finally got to Gina, the smell of fish. Otherwise, in a bad light, you could actually pass for me. If you had a sense of style."

The insults had little effect. As long as Cenzo could hold on to the possibility that Giulia had escaped, he was impervious to his brother's sniping.

"What do you want?" Cenzo asked.

"Peace on earth, like everyone else. Well, not everyone. Sheer momentum will carry us to a final bloodbath."

"So now you're anti-Mussolini?"

"Mussolini doesn't matter. Hitler is calling the shots now and he is totally mad."

"Don't tell me, tell the Germans."

"I have many times."

Giorgio stood as a Wehrmacht colonel entered the bar. He was an older man, dignified in profile, even though abrasions scarred the left side of his head. Cenzo remembered that his name was Steiner. He had been the senior officer on the gunboat the night that Cenzo dropped the SS lieutenant Hoff down a well.

"The fisherman Vianello," the colonel said, and gave Cenzo a nod.

"Colonel."

Steiner and Giorgio shook hands. It seemed they knew each other.

"Do you mind?" The colonel pulled up a chair and placed a well-worn leather satchel on the next table. "Do you remember the debate with Lieutenant Hoff over the marine chart? The two of you did not get along as I recall. Cigarette?"

"Thank you."

"A Camel." The colonel lit it for him. "Nothing but the best for my friends. Nido doesn't recognize me, but I used to come here as a young man to listen to his stories. He served the most volatile grappa in Italy. Does he still?"

"Yes."

"Good, something we can depend on."

Cenzo wondered about the scar on Steiner's face. It was not so much a noble souvenir left by a saber at a military academy as it was the gritty erasure left by a hand grenade, with the hair crisped and the ear a buckshot gray. And when the colonel lit a cigarette for himself, Cenzo detected a stiffness in his arm and torso as if those parts were held together by a leather harness.

"Vianello is a local name, isn't it? I remember there were only about four last names in this entire village: Vianello, Boscolo, Scarpa, and Busetto. We played a friendly football match with them and it was impossible to keep the players straight. It's not totally unlike the war between German soldiers and partisans."

So far, neither Colonel Steiner nor Giorgio had mentioned Giulia or Russo, although Cenzo felt a cold worm of fear in his gut.

"I'm sorry, I don't see the connection," Cenzo said.

"Well, you're right," Steiner said. "There's no reason to dwell on the past. We have to think about the future, and the future is slipping away. Say there were a few sane and sober men on both sides of a conflict. How would they know each other?"

"I have no idea," Cenzo said.

"They'd need a messenger. Sometimes an unlikely messenger is the best. Vittorio Silber was my messenger. He brought me information from the Americans."

"Are you a spy?"

"Let's say I'm gathering information that would hopefully bring about an early peace."

"What's Giorgio's part in all this?"

"Giorgio is just helping me get to you."

Cenzo looked at the soldiers standing guard at the door. They were veterans who leaned into the conversation.

"Who do these men report to?" Cenzo asked.

"They report only to me."

"And who do you report to?"

"I can't tell you any more than that. All I can say is that men on either side have to put aside not only their differences and ideologies but personal enmity. Unfortunately, enmity between brothers is sometimes the hardest to give up. Psychologically, hatred between brothers can be more delicious than ending a war."

"You've lost me."

"I need Giulia Silber. You did the world a great favor in killing Lieutenant Hoff. He was a mad dog. I know that she was on your fishing boat, but I've lost her and I need your help to get her back. To do this, I requested the help of your brother Giorgio. He has agreed. You must too."

"Why would I?"

"Because if you won't, you will end up like your friend Russo." From his tunic the colonel produced a postcard-size photograph of Eusebio Russo. Cenzo winced in spite of himself. The face in the picture was beaten to a pulp and there was no doubt he was dead. "The penalty for murdering an SS officer is quick and severe."

"Did the SS do this?" Cenzo asked.

"The Italian SS or the German SS. This photograph surfaced in Salò, although that doesn't mean that the girl is in Salò or even that she is alive. Anyway, the German SS has blamed Hoff's death on Russo. It's a tidy way of handling things while making themselves appear competent."

"Since when do Germans concern themselves with the fate of a Jewish girl?"

"It's in everybody's interest. Whether she knows it or not, she can help identify the man who betrayed Silber and his wife."

"Are they dead?" Cenzo asked.

"Yes, I'm afraid so. There are Germans and there are Germans, just as there are the sane and the insane. If the war goes on, there will be needless killing on both sides. I, like Silber, would like to see an early peace. The man who betrayed them will do anything to prevent it."

"And I should trust you?"

"We have to trust each other."

"Giorgio and I do not have a good history."

"So, would you put personal spite ahead of the life of this girl and many others?"

"I didn't say that."

"Then what *did* you say?"

"I'll work with anyone else."

"No one else has your brother's entrée into different circles in Salò. German or Italian, he's popular with them all."

"I'm a film star," Giorgio said.

"And what am I supposed to be?" Cenzo asked.

"Your brother's toady. Don't worry, there are many superfluous people in the film world," Steiner said.

"In Milan?"

"In Salò. That is where we think the girl is now."

Giorgio said, "We will put the net where the fish are. You should understand the concept."

"No."

"You're turning us down?" Steiner said.

"I told you he wouldn't do it," Giorgio said.

"What about the girl?" Steiner asked.

"If she was with Russo, she's probably as dead as he is," Cenzo said. "What makes you think I care?"

The colonel opened the satchel on the next table and took out one of Cenzo's sketches of Giulia. Black hair framed a pale face and a subdued light lent life and depth to her eyes.

Steiner said, "Not the *Mona Lisa*, but not bad for an amateur. At the very least I would say it was drawn with some intimacy."

Cenzo turned to Giorgio. "You took the colonel to my fishing shack?"

"Blame me," Steiner said. "I had to learn as much about you as I could."

"Actually, you'd be a fish out of water in Salò, if you will pardon the expression," Giorgio said.

Steiner said, "There are people Giorgio can

132

introduce you to. Besides, he needs someone he can trust."

"Me?"

"I'd put money on it," the colonel said. "Will you help us?"

"You mean lure her out?"

"That's another way of putting it. Remember that while we're looking for the man who betrayed her father, that man will be looking for her."

There was a voice at the door of the bar. "I am Squadron Leader Farina. I understand you have the anti-Fascist agitator Innocenzo Vianello inside. I demand an opportunity to denounce him."

Steiner looked toward Cenzo for a decision. Yes? No? Finally, Cenzo delivered the faintest of nods.

At a signal from Colonel Steiner the soldiers allowed Squadron Leader Farina to step in and deliver a stiff salute. "I am denouncing the fisherman Innocenzo Vianello for spreading defeatist propaganda and undermining the fighting spirit of Pellestrina. I also want it noted that I was the first to uncover his treacherous activities."

"Too late," Giorgio said. "I already have."

14

The Stork reconnaissance plane was a lightweight masterpiece of wood, aluminum, and stainless steel, with a high forward canopy and oversized wings. The instrumentation was basic: fuel gauge, airspeed, altimeter, and turn-and-bank indicator. Giorgio was at the controls and the plane rose from thermal to thermal as if climbing stairs.

Although Cenzo expected a formation of Mustangs to drop from the clouds with cannons blazing, none did. He made out 88mm antiaircraft batteries draped in camouflage netting on the ground. The Stork rose and fell with the contours of the land and he felt like a fly waiting to be slapped. Each mountain village seemed to claim a zigzag road, the stone pile of a castle, a church with a memorial statue of the Great War, when Italy had been on the winning side. Dirt roads ran as rivulets from town to town. Each farm had a roof of red tiles, a cow pen, a pigsty, or a small vineyard framed by lemon groves and oaks and the dusty clime of the Italian Socialist Republic. German Occupied Italy, to be more exact, stretched from Tuscany north to the Swiss border. The black smoke of an armored train slid underneath the plane as it disappeared into the contours of the landscape. Soldiers riding the tops of the first and last cars trained their machine guns on the plane just in case.

The German army had two hundred thousand veteran troops in Italy. Mussolini had fifty thousand hard-core Fascists. Together they controlled Milan, Turin, Genoa and Verona and Salò, the new capitol of the German Republic. The war was lost, but it wasn't over.

The flight lasted no more than half an hour before Monte Baldo, a remnant of the Ice Age, seemed to rise like a single boulder over Lake Garda. At its base the villas and gardens were as charming as a scene made of marzipan. It was "Paradise on Earth," inspiration for a million postcards that featured sailboats, paddleboats, palms and poplars, poetry and romance. But what had been holiday traffic was now replaced by military half-ton trucks, ambulances, and black sedans with German flags on their fenders.

"Don't be clever, don't be smart," Giorgio said and turned in his seat to Cenzo. "Publicly, you're looking for your niece Giulia Vianello, an eighteen-year-old girl from Pellestrina. Also for your friend Eusebio Russo, a fishmonger who unfortunately is dead. Maybe Russo was involved in the black market and a bit of an agitator. Tread carefully. As for Silber and Colonel Steiner, you'll probably fuck up, so don't say anything unless I directly tell you to. We'll meet some people on the ground who will talk as if they know all about conspiracies and invite you to share your opinions. All the more reason to keep your mouth shut. And about Gina, say nothing at all."

Giorgio eased down and as soon as the Stork's pontoons touched water he cut the engine and let the plane coast to a dock where two deckhands secured it with ropes. The Salò marina was full of pleasure boats nodding by the dock but going nowhere. A pair of mechanics helped Giorgio out of the Stork. It was obvious from their welcome that they held him in awe; after all, here was a man who virtually tilted with dragons.

A woman leaning against a red Alfa Romeo convertible waved and called, "Giorgio! Giorgio, over here!"

She was in a tailored suit and silk scarf that stamped her as possessing money and style. A round man in a white suit filled the car's passenger seat and held on to his hat like a squirrel with a nut.

"Oh my God, and who is this?" the woman asked.

"My brother, Cenzo," Giorgio said.

"*The* brother?"

"I'm afraid so," Cenzo said.

Giorgio sighed. "This is Signora Maria Paz, the wife of the former Argentine consul. Maria often speaks before she thinks."

Maria Paz was in her late thirties, an athletic woman with bangles on her wrist and a hint of carnal knowledge to her smile. Cenzo could picture her at the head of a conga line. Her eyes darted back and forth from brother to brother.

"It's hard to believe," she said.

"And this is the movie producer Otto Klein," Giorgio said.

Otto doffed his hat. "A virtual doppelgänger! A double."

Not really, Cenzo thought. He had darker eyes and unruly hair, and was broader through the chest from lifting heavy nets and crates.

"You just came in from . . . ?" asked Otto Klein.

"Venice," Giorgio said.

"And . . ." Otto hesitated.

"It's still there."

"I didn't doubt it. I didn't doubt it for a minute."

"Poor Otto, he's so nervous," Maria said.

Klein said, "I only want it understood that I'm Swiss. I'm neutral."

"I understand." She kissed his cheek and made him blush. "I'm not sure that General Eisenhower will." To Cenzo she said, "Welcome to Salò. Alas we have sunshine, which means that Milan and Verona will have a clear sky for bombing."

"I heard that Storks were Rommel's favorite recon plane, but I never knew they came outfitted with pontoons," Otto Klein said.

"I had one modified," said Giorgio.

"Very chic," said Maria Paz.

She drove with careless abandon along the shore

of Lake Garda. Giorgio sat up front with Maria, Cenzo in back with Klein. Side by side, the town's Mediterranean villas possessed the elegance of a *corps de ballet*. The Villa Acquarone, its Palladian arches draped with a swastika, had become German headquarters. The Hotel Monte Baldo had been commandeered by German medical staff and the classical Villa Alba had been taken over by German radio. But was Salò Rome? Was it Venice? Berlin? Even the Orologio, the clock tower of Salò, looked more like an item of furniture than the gateway to a world capital.

The presence of the Argentine consul's wife suggested that Salò had maintained a diplomatic community and a stylish one at that. It was, after all, the capital of the Italian Socialist Republic, the RSI, a puppet regime but a regime nonetheless.

"I've packed you a suitcase," Giorgio said to Cenzo. "Your own clothes are only appropriate for fishing. I've left you shaving gear too."

Klein had a pink complexion and yellowish hair that stuck out the back of his neck like damp feathers. He tapped Cenzo on the knee.

"Ufa."

"Excuse me?" Cenzo said.

"I'm with Ufa, the German movie studio. Actually, I'm in charge of distribution of German films in foreign countries. We're not doing very much of that these days. You've probably seen our films. Historical dramas. Grandeur. Have you seen *The Titanic*? Our latest. I like a movie with wherewithal and I'm always on the lookout for a pretty face. What I'd give for another Marlene."

"They're hard to find," Giorgio said.

"Otto is sometimes an actor himself," Maria said.

Klein said, "I wouldn't go that far. *Amateur Hour*, that sort of thing. Newsreels are the hardest, and these days newsreels are impossible."

"I agree," said Maria. "One day you're marching around the Eiffel Tower, the next day, Berlin is an empty shell."

"These are temporary setbacks," Klein said. "The next few days will clarify the situation. Giorgio and I haven't had our final say, have we, Giorgio? Believe me, this war is far from over."

"Is that true?" Cenzo asked Giorgio. "You're going to save Mussolini? Are you a magician too?"

A column of German infantry made a hollow thumping as they marched along the wooden boards of the promenade that ran along the lake. They were disciplined, and for an army that was supposed to be on the brink of collapse, they looked well organized and ready to fight on. But a person never could tell. Everyone knew stories about whole battalions that fought to the last man rather than surrender, and other battalions that searched for Allied troops to surrender to.

The German troops were followed by ragtag groups of the Italian Fascist state: an imitation army, Blackshirts, police, carabinieri.

Maria turned to Cenzo. "Do you like it? This parade was supposed to boost morale. Everyone but fanatics is leaving Salò. My husband and I are all that's left of the diplomatic corps. Why are you here? Bad timing?"

"I'm looking for a niece, Giulia Vianello. She's missing."

"Have you buried your differences with Giorgio to find this young girl? Bravo."

"It would make a good film," Klein said.

"Good film, bad film, and the hell with morals," Maria said.

"Look who's getting virtuous."

"I don't think the word 'virtuous' has any meaning anymore," Maria said. "Not for a woman, not in a war."

Klein said, "What would really boost our morale is more rain so the Allies have less visibility and can't bomb us into the ground. Foul weather is what we're after."

"But you're still Swiss, right?" Giorgio said.

Once the parade passed, the cafés returned to normal. Handsome officers strolled with attractive nurses. Waiters carried trays full of Campari and seltzer water. Bureaucrats in black shirts carried black satchels.

"I wonder how many of these self-important

men are ready to cast aside the black shirts and find their old serge suits," Maria said.

"You must have a uniform in the back of your closet," Cenzo said to Giorgio.

"My good friend Giorgio is an exception," Klein said. "He would have advanced in heaven or hell."

"What does she look like, this Giulia?" Maria asked.

Cenzo said, "Small and dark."

"That's ninety percent of girls in Italy."

"She's well educated."

"Can she speak any languages?"

"English and French."

"She doesn't sound like a fisherman's daughter, does she?"

"Her parents were professionals."

"Ah, that must explain it."

Giorgio had reserved second-floor digs for Cenzo in the Hotel Golfo, a sickly-green establishment with a flat façade. Maria Paz and her Alfa Romeo had gone on their way. Otto Klein waited downstairs for a business meeting with Giorgio. As Klein put it, there wasn't room for three men in such a hole.

Giorgio set a leather suitcase on the bed. "Decent clothes. We can't have you running around Salò looking like a fisherman. The main thing is that you're only a block from the lake and you have a private bath."

"Why were Maria and Klein part of the welcoming committee?"

"You liked Maria?"

"I liked her well enough."

"You thought she was a good soul?"

"Why not?"

"Well, she knows everyone. She also makes a mean martini." Giorgio planted a room key in Cenzo's hand. "Maria will come back for you. I have to do some business with Herr Klein for an hour or so. He still thinks there's time for one last cinematic epic. If you leave, steer clear of the other tenants of the Hotel Golfo. They're lunatics, especially the Black Brigade. Best not to talk to any of them." As he shut the door, Giorgio added, "Don't screw up."

Alone for the first time, Cenzo looked around the room, not that there was much to see. The rich did not treat their staff with luxury. Peeling walls were decorated with a mirror, prints of the lake, a crucifix, and a plaster Virgin. A bureau with four drawers was empty except for loose change and spare buttons. An armoire with no hangers but a pile of blankets. A thin mattress without pillow or sheets. A miniature bathroom with a shower that squeaked and dripped. A shaving mirror hung from a hook. Giorgio's suitcase, however, looked extravagantly expensive, and the shirts bore his monogram *GGV* for Giorgio "Giovanni" Vianello. The middle name was always given by the church and the name for boys in Pellestrina was always Giovanni. There was one small window. Otherwise, the room was as airless as a tomb.

Cenzo washed and shaved, and as he rinsed his razor a rhythmic creaking of bedsprings started to come from the next room. It was hard to believe anyone's amorous spirit could outdo the grimness of the setting. Cenzo went for a cigarette on the fire escape at the end of the hall.

He had no idea of how to search for Giulia. He knew only that he was out of his depth. He knew nothing about the German army, partisans, or the surreal world of Salò.

Colonel Steiner said that Russo had been found dead. Murdered. Alone. This was the point at which all certainties were reexamined. What had happened to the second man in Russo's boat? Was his friend Russo actually a partisan or was he an informant? Why had he gotten off with only a black eye the first time and then killed the second? Who could say that Giulia had not suffered Russo's fate? She may have talked her way out of the same situation. She was one terrific talker. One assumption he had to make was that Giulia was alive.

The fire-escape door opened and a man dressed entirely in black stepped outside to wipe sweat from his brow. He could have been a neighborhood butcher, with a potbelly, cheeks as round as a teapot, and a little duster of a mustache. If he was surprised at encountering company, he didn't show it. He studied Cenzo.

"Vianello?"

"Yes."

"But not *the* Vianello."

"The other Vianello."

" 'The other'? That shows modesty." The man nodded as if he had touched on a universal truth. Cenzo couldn't put a name to him right away but he had seen his face on the sort of posters that encouraged Fascist allegiance. The man shrugged apologetically at his apron. "One should never be afraid to get his hands dirty in the service of Il Duce."

"Do you know my brother?"

"Giorgio Vianello? I know *of* him. Have you come like a good brother to assist him?"

Orsini was the man's name, Cenzo remembered. Commander Orsini, leader of the Black Brigade, returned the smile. The Black Brigade was the fist of the Italian Fascist state. That Orsini even knew of Cenzo's existence was unsettling.

"Family honor," Cenzo said.

"Yes. 'Home, Motherland, Honor.' " Orsini looked as if he would slap Cenzo on the back with approval. "Maybe you would consider joining us?"

"Joining the Black Brigade?"

"You know our motto: 'Embrace death.' "

Cenzo was saved by the return of Maria Paz in

her red convertible. "Making new friends?" she called. "I see you have found Commander Orsini. I hope I'm interrupting you."

"The Whore of Babylon," Orsini muttered as he slipped away into the hall.

"Such charm," Maria said when Cenzo joined her. "He can't stand the fact that he can't threaten me. He wouldn't dare. Anyway, your brother has given me the assignment of entertaining you. Much better. This way I can give you the lowdown."

15

Maria drove with the air of an older sister. Her lipstick and fingernails were candy red and she blew kisses to German motorcycles buzzing past.

"Such brave boys," she said. "Fighting for a lost cause, but very brave."

"And confused," Cenzo said.

"Salò is the ultimate confusion, like having different operas take place on the same stage at the same time."

"What else does Giorgio have planned for me besides throwing me in the water like a bucket of chum?"

"I can't believe Giorgio put you in the same hotel as Orsini."

"Then you don't know my brother. What's happening tonight?"

"We're having dinner with General Kassel. You should be honored. After all, he has just been made commander of German forces on the Western Front. The general has commanded Giorgio and Otto Klein to be there and Giorgio has commanded me likewise."

"Giorgio can command the wife of the Argentine consul?"

"He can be very persuasive. Besides, we have no official consulate here anymore."

"And what would I have to say to the general tonight?"

"Fishing. Talk about fishing. Generals love to fish. Churchill fished here. The *crème de la crème*. Before the war, this was a destination of German tourists who fished in straw hats and white jackets. Now it's helmets and Wehrmacht green." She waved dark thoughts aside and pointed out to the Villa Feltrinelli. "This is the height of domesticity, where Mussolini's wife, Signora Rachele, lives. And up the road is the Villa Fiordaliso, the romantic tower where he meets his mistress, Claretta."

"Aren't the villas dangerously close together?"

"Yes. God forbid the wife and mistress ever meet face-to-face. It's the job of the German SS to keep them apart. Do you know how embarrassing it is for a fearsome SS officer to watch over a henhouse? Claretta is young and spry. Rachele is older but tough, a bulldog. It would be a good fight."

"The idea amuses you."

"Except when I see something like that." She pointed to a poster on the casino that showed a mother telling her son, "I Would Rather You Came Home a Dead Patriot Than a Live Traitor." Maria said, "No mother on earth would say that. This worship of death is sick."

"If you feel that way, why aren't you back in Buenos Aires?"

"A diplomat goes where he's ordered. My husband was sent here, and now, unfortunately, he's unable to travel."

"What if Salò is bombed?"

"It won't be. At least it hasn't been."

"Why not? Mussolini is here."

"It would be a waste of ammunition. Ask yourself: Which is more important, Mussolini or a locomotive. It's sad."

"What is?"

"Il Duce. He's practically a prisoner. He has Germans watching him all the time. You'll see him riding his bicycle or sneaking off to see his mistress or hiding from his wife." She pointed at more sites as they passed. "Here we have German Headquarters, a small Parthenon for German radio, cozy villas for the police and Black Brigade, a German hospital for amputations next to a crematorium for limbs. Convenient. Then there's the latest gossip. *Amour, amour, amour.* Goebbels has a lover in Budapest. Hitler loves his dog Blondi. But enough of war. What are you doing in Salò? Please don't give me a fairy tale about a runaway teenager. The girl might be distraught, but why would she leave Venice for Salò? On the other hand, a man well might track down the brother who seduced his wife. That I find entirely believable."

"This wasn't my idea."

"Well, be careful. You look far too honorable. That is a handicap in Salò."

"As soon as I find the girl, I'll go back to Pellestrina."

"Not too soon. You're invited to a party."

"I think I'll pass."

"You can't. It's Hitler's birthday and you're invited."

The officers mess was hung with blackout curtains and larger-than-life-size portraits of Hitler and Mussolini. A quartet of musicians selected from the ranks played a relentless stream of waltzes. It was a golden evening. Officers wore their dress uniforms and dined in the company of adoring nurses and secretaries, for tomorrow might bring orders to the Eastern Front.

Compared to other women, Maria was a red rose among sprigs of edelweiss. Meanwhile, Otto

Klein sweated like a man on trial and Cenzo and General Kassel discussed fishing. The general was especially interested in spearing octopus in the Greek manner.

Cenzo explained, "You have to see an octopus blink, otherwise you won't see it at all."

"And the fish called 'goby.' I've heard so much about that."

"But don't see because it disappears magically in your risotto."

"Too bad we don't have time to fish some of the streams here," the general said. He was a professional soldier, a blue-eyed warrior with an Iron Cross tied by a ribbon around his neck. "Did you know that the violin was invented in Salò? Remarkable place."

A major as round as Goering got to his feet and tapped his glass until everyone hushed.

"Gentlemen, ladies, let me propose a toast to our beloved Führer on this, his wonderful birthday. Here is a man for the ages who has remade the modern world, led the German people to greatness, and even now is all that stands between civilization and a pit of bestiality. To Adolf Hitler, *Sieg Heil, Sieg Heil, Sieg Heil*!"

With no ado, Kassel resumed his seat. "Ah, here is our food. Not risotto, perhaps, but good German fare all the same." A waiter served lake trout and potatoes doused with vinegar. "Soon enough they will have a different clientele. They'll be serving steak and Coca-Cola. Klein, what are you so nervous about?"

"He talked to Goebbels," Giorgio said.

"What about?" Kassel was immediately wary.

"The film."

"Not that again."

"I'm afraid so. He was still filming as of last week."

The general's chin sank onto his chest. "There we were, trying to hold the line against a foe that vastly outnumbered us, and Goebbels insisted on making a movie about the *Titanic*, as if that would inspire us. He demanded a thousand men as extras and sets to blow up while Hamburg was being leveled for real."

"He said it will be the film to end all films," Klein said. "Of course, all movie producers say that."

"We should strip Herr Goebbels," said Kassel, "paint his ass red, and let him run in front of the American Fifth Army." The room went quiet. "Of course, I would never suggest such a thing, not as long as I have our friend Klein on guard like a canary in a mine."

Giorgio said, "Let us help. Given arms, Italian fighters are willing to fight to the end."

"You know I can't do that. I am fond of you, Giorgio. You are very entertaining, but my troops must move intact as a fighting unit."

"Meaning that Italians can't fight?" Giorgio asked.

The general shrugged.

"Italy has the best fighter plane in the war," Giorgio said. "We shot down 150 Allied airplanes. We would have shot down many more had we been given the planes or parachutes."

"Yes, yes, for you it's a matter of honor. As a soldier, I understand. But for me, it's a matter of strategy. Brother Cenzo, what is it like under the stars on the Venice Lagoon? What's the biggest fish you ever saw?"

"An anchovy. Before it split into ten thousand fish."

The general wagged his fork. "Giorgio, your brother is deeper than he first appears."

"He fools people," Giorgio said.

The general dropped his voice. "I am riding my horse Metropol one last time tomorrow. You understand what I'm saying. Soon I will not be able to guarantee your safety in Salò. Even diplomatic status may not be enough, Maria. As for Metropol, he may soon be on the menu here. So let's enjoy the moment. Cenzo, you seem a good fellow. Why are you here?"

"I'm looking for my niece, Giulia Vianello, from Venice. She might be in the hands of the army or the police."

"A young girl adrift in the middle of war? Her chances are not good."

Cenzo dug in his billfold and showed the general his pencil sketch of Giulia.

"I'm sorry," Kassel said. "Frankly, she looks like a lot of other Italian girls. I'll alert my staff. Who knows? Now, friends, I bid you adieu."

Kassel pushed his chair back, and as he stood, every officer stood as well. An aide brought a coat and cap.

"Be prepared," the general said. "History does not treat losers kindly."

When Kassel was out the door, Maria said, "So there you have it. Our all-powerful general can't save his army, or his horse, or a girl."

Cenzo asked, "When were all those Allied planes shot down?"

"During the Milan raids six months ago. I was there," Klein said. "It was brutal."

"Did you know my wife, Gina?"

Perhaps it was bad manners or too early to mention one's dead wife, Cenzo thought, because the pause that followed was long and awkward.

"Pardon?" Klein said.

Cenzo said, "Her name was Angelina but ever since she was a little girl she called herself Gina. Even then, she thought a short name would look better on a theater marquee. Do you remember her?"

Although Cenzo thought he had asked the question amicably enough, the rest of the table held its breath.

"I remember, but why do you even mention her?" Maria asked.

"Cuckold's rights," he said. "Curiosity."

"I thought you came to find another girl," Giorgio said.

"You know how it is: sometimes you find more than one fish on your line."

They walked along the promenade, Maria Paz keeping the peace between the brothers and Otto Klein behind, practicing his excuses to Goebbels. They passed 20mm gun emplacements manned by soldiers who snapped to attention. Buoy lights floated on the water while the oppressive rock called San Bartolomeo threatened to roll across the lake and snuff out Salò.

Otto said, "Interior shot. Day. There was a suitcase on the landing of a flight of stairs. Gina was supposed to run up the steps, pick up the suitcase, and run down. Unfortunately, that was when the bomb came through the roof. That was it. Bad luck."

"Where were you?" Cenzo asked Giorgio.

Giorgio sighed. "I was in another room. It was her scene."

"Why weren't you all in the bomb shelter? Didn't you hear the air raid alarm go off?"

"The British bombed all night and the Americans all day but not in that part of Milan, and the director decided to go ahead," Otto said. "The scene shouldn't have taken more than a minute. It's ironic. The set was built to resemble a bombed-out house. The bomb came right through the open roof."

"Was anyone else injured?" asked Cenzo.

"The director, cameraman, light man, sound-man, and two stage crew were all killed," Giorgio said.

"Who survived besides you?"

"No one," said Giorgio.

"What sort of injuries did you have?"

"A concussion, nothing else. Are you done?"

"Not yet. What did you mean, 'the scene should have taken no more than a minute'?"

"Gina had trouble hitting her marks where she should stop or go. It's complicated for a newcomer."

"How much time did it take her?"

"Five minutes, maybe ten."

"To go up the stairs, pick up a suitcase, and come down?"

"I could only show her so many times. I think she got discouraged."

"You 'think'? Didn't you see her?"

"I stepped away to take the pressure off her."

"What was in the suitcase?"

"This is getting ridiculous. A couple of books, probably. She was playing a girl who was leaving a ruined house. She wasn't supposed to be taking much."

Klein caught up. "It was terribly tragic. The studio was going to promote her as our new ingénue.

This was going to be her screen debut. As it was, the film was never finished."

"Are you satisfied?" Maria asked Cenzo.

Giorgio said, "I don't want to bruise your feelings, but Gina didn't love you. I didn't seduce her. She was ready to leave."

Cenzo's brain searched for a way to deny such an obvious explanation. Thinking about Gina drove him crazy. It was interesting that thinking about Giulia kept him sane. It wasn't clear whether he was in over his head or "just smart enough to fool the fish," as his father used to say.

16

In the morning, dressed in his work clothes and boots, Cenzo walked along the Salò–Brescia road. German convoys eyed him as they rumbled past, and a carload of the Black Brigade sped by close enough to make him jump off the road. Finally, he left the road and climbed a field of grapes that had shriveled on the vine. A couple hundred meters down was a farm with a tiled roof and pigsty. The day was cool but the hike had left him sweating. Sitting in the shade of an oak tree, he waited.

A dog came out of the house and nosed around the ground in hopes of scraps. A cat emerged, sneered at the dog, and curled up on a cool spot.

Then they went back in the house at the same moment, so somebody was home.

The drone of flies nearly put Cenzo to sleep. He had brought a cloth cap and a bandana to cool his neck. He watched the long, stiff ears of a hare quiver among the vines. Cenzo didn't understand Giorgio's relationship with Maria Paz. They seemed to be friends rather than lovers. And, of course, there was Giorgio's relationship with Gina. Perhaps, Cenzo conceded, that was a relationship that he refused to understand. He pictured Gina on the movie set as she climbed the stairs to the suitcase. A certain exasperation had crept into Giorgio's voice when he described how she had missed her mark. Well, who was she? A waitress? An heiress? What was her role in the movie? It seemed strange that everyone else on the set had died. Six other people. That was a large bomb. And the death of a promising ingénue? That must have been in the Milan newspaper.

The hare bolted as a woman emerged from the house with a basket of clothes and pinned them to the line. Cenzo knew he was bait. That was his role.

Cenzo imagined the bomb hurtling through the open roof. Had Giorgio crawled through the rubble to get to Gina? Was she dead when he reached her or did she die in his arms? Had she said anything?

A lark's song drifted across the hill. The bird

performed like a virtuoso going up and down the scale. Cenzo ignored an ant tickling his arm. As an oak twig snapped, the lark flew off close to the ground. Cenzo heard another footstep and looked up into the barrel of a shotgun.

Four men in baggy pants, loose shirts, and caps moved across a terrain of pines. All but Cenzo wore red bandanas on their arms.

A veteran the others called "the Spaniard" walked alongside Cenzo and explained in a Madrileño accent, "Luckily for you, we are the Garibaldi Group. Not bandits but true patriots. Most of us are communists, but not all. We have peasants and professors, intellectuals and workers, and when the war is over we will go our different ways. Until then, we must practice solidarity."

"How long have you been at this?"

"Almost ten years now. Madrid, Barcelona, and Gijón. Our worst enemy has always been infiltrators. We treat them roughly for their sake, because for every one we execute, we discourage that many more."

"Cigarette?" Cenzo offered him one.

"Thank you." The Spaniard put it in his shirt pocket. "You should save one for yourself."

"Why?"

"For your execution." The Spaniard studied him. "You're not afraid, are you?"

"I'm looking for someone."

"I hope they're worth it."

It was a curious thing, Cenzo thought, but he was not afraid. He was living moment to moment, his senses heightened. He wished he had his paints and brushes to capture the partisans as they pushed through the woods.

So far as he could tell, they were taking him to meet their commander, a man called Dante whom they described as a poet in his own right. Among themselves, they used nicknames; besides the Spaniard, there were Caruso, Peppino, and Piola. Caruso had been in the chorus of an opera company and found it difficult to hike without humming. Peppino and Piola were no more than fifteen years old, runners who took information from one partisan group to another. The boys cast covert glances at Cenzo, obviously anxious about having to pull the trigger on him.

"They don't understand that everybody's nervous," the Spaniard said. "That's why in executions they have the prisoner face away. Nobody wants to kill anyone face-to-face. Unless they're sitting in a chair."

"Which do you prefer if you were to be shot?" Cenzo asked.

The Spaniard shrugged. "It makes no difference to me either way as long as the man is a good shot."

"What about the last rites?"

"I like it. It gives the affair a nice formality.

Also, we're bound to make mistakes, but with a priest you feel you're putting someone directly into the hands of God. Right now we have more infiltrators all the time, because the war is coming to an end and many Fascists are trying to switch sides. Like snakes from a fire. Dante barely has time to deal with them, so he's less inclined to give them long trials. Can I give you some advice? Be brief and be quiet. What were you doing sitting out there under a tree anyway?"

"Trying to attract attention."

"It worked."

Cenzo did not ask the usual questions to get his bearings, because the usual questions could get a man killed. The party walked for an hour until the pine needles and bracken cleared, and they entered an encampment of men with red bandanas on their arms. They lounged on boxes of hand grenades, packs of plastique explosive, and chickens in a cage. Some of the men cleaned rifles, some played chess, one was immersed in the comic book exploits of Rin Tin Tin: *The Wonder Dog*.

The Spaniard handed Cenzo's papers to a professorial type with rimless glasses who sat by himself against a tree trunk and jotted in a notebook. His hair flew this way and that, like an egret's, and Cenzo knew without being told this was Dante.

"We found him at a farm near the road to Salò,"

the Spaniard said. "He says he's searching for his niece and he hopes we will help him find her."

"In the middle of a war zone?"

"That's what he says."

Dante went through Cenzo's papers, pausing at "Occupation: Fisherman" to look at Cenzo's hands, and stopped at Cenzo's family name. "Vianello? Are you related to Vianello the actor?"

"He's my brother."

"And you dare to come here? Your brother is a Fascist agent. You're begging to be shot."

"I'm looking for a girl named Giulia. She was traveling from Venice with a friend, Eusebio Russo. He might not have made it and she is missing."

"Or she turned him in," said Dante.

"She's eighteen years old."

"We have fighters younger than that. And traitors too."

"She's Jewish."

"But you're not."

"That's right."

"So you're not her uncle. You lied about that."

"She escaped from the Germans. I took her in."

"How did she escape?"

"She swam across the lagoon."

"Nobody swims across the lagoon."

"Byron did."

Dante's stare gave way to a smile and he closed his notebook. "So they say."

"That's impossible," the Spaniard said.

"Not only impossible, but in iambic tetrameter," Dante said. " 'She walks in beauty, like the night / Of cloudless climes and starry skies . . .' Perhaps it should have been 'She swims in beauty . . .' "

"Perhaps," Cenzo said.

Dante took off his glasses and rubbed the bridge of his nose. Cenzo got a sense of how exhausted the partisan leader was, not only physically but in spirit.

"And you say you knew Eusebio Russo?" Dante asked.

"We served in the army together in Abyssinia."

"You knew he might be a partisan or else you wouldn't have asked us to help you with the girl."

"I thought he might be."

"Might be a member of the Garibaldi Group?"

"Yes."

"Might be a Red?"

"Yes."

"But you are not."

"No."

"Then how did you know which farm to stop at and which tree to sit under?"

"It was a tree you could see like a billboard, and when the woman hung her laundry, that was as good as a sign."

"Did you know that the Germans pulled Russo in for interrogation?"

"I was told that," Cenzo said.

"And then released him?"

"I had heard he was dead."

"That's interesting," said Dante.

They were interrupted by a chicken that escaped its cage and comically ran from partisan to partisan, in and out of the radio hut and around the ammo cases, until the boy called Peppino caught it and cut off its head.

The Spaniard approved. "One stroke. The boy is learning."

Dinner was boiled chicken and bread served in American mess kits. The partisans sat close to Dante like dogs around their master.

"The Americans are generous," he told Cenzo. "They drop tommy guns, and ammunition, chocolate bars, cigarettes, even explosives wrapped in mattresses. A thoughtful people. I could write about them the way Homer wrote about the ancient Greeks and make a fortune in Hollywood, but I can't because I'm a communist. Besides, they'll probably do it themselves. The Russians have agitprop, the Germans have Goebbels, and Mussolini has Giorgio Vianello, the 'Lion of Tripoli.' Tell me, seriously, what do you think of your brother's acting? Family pride aside."

"I'd say it's competent."

"Such a carefully chosen word. Usually when people discuss film they use words like 'exciting,' 'romantic,' or 'overwhelming.' You say 'competent.'"

"I'm not a film critic."

"Why not? Mussolini is. Hitler is. Stalin is too. Everybody's a film critic. There is no love lost between you and your brother, is there?" Dante rubbed his face. "It's important to protect Italy from the kind of scoundrels and mountebanks it's suffered in the past. Do you agree?"

"I suppose so."

"It demands decisive action. Sentiment cannot be allowed to get in the way."

Cenzo took a moment to understand. "You want me to kill Giorgio?"

"And do the world a favor. Your brother is a difficult man to get close to. You can do it."

"And put a knife in his back?"

"Or a bullet in his head." Dante handed Cenzo a 9mm Beretta. "I won't pretend it would be a noble act, but it is a necessary one." Dante looked up as lights passed in the sky, accompanied by antiaircraft fire. "See, the rest of the world is celebrating. Like a parade in hell."

Dante discoursed on Russian literature, Japanese prints, American dynamism. He put Cenzo in mind of a record spinning faster and faster as the evening wore on. Every time Cenzo brought up Giulia or Russo, Dante changed the subject.

Finally, as darkness fell, Dante said, "You know, a month from now, you and I might be strolling in a liberated Venice. It will be like the day after Carnival when all the masks come off and it will become evident who are the heroes, who are the traitors, and who are the innocent victims. I think there will be many surprises, some quite sad. Your friend Russo, for example, may not have been the hero you thought he was."

"Who saw him?" Cenzo asked.

"I can't say."

A more startling idea occurred to Cenzo. "Is he still alive?"

"I can't say that either. All I can say is that, for a dead man, he's been very busy on the black market."

17

A black sedan was waiting when Cenzo returned to his room at the Hotel Golfo. Two Blackshirts leaned against the car's fender like lizards basking in the sun. One snapped a cigarette butt at Cenzo's heels.

Upstairs, Party Leader Orsini didn't seem to find it unusual at all to be sitting on Cenzo's bed, looking through the contents of his suitcases. He looked like a man who simply enjoyed gathering information the way a philatelist collected stamps. His uniform was black and trim, his mustache modest yet dapper, and he balanced his cap on his knee.

"The door was open," Orsini said.

"So you came in."

"Yes." He flourished a pink note and envelope. "These were under the door too. I hope you don't find it obtrusive if I read it?"

"I think you already have."

"'Dear Cenzo, Where have you been? I will pick you up at six. No excuses. *Un beso*, Maria.' So everyone wants to know: Where have you been?"

"I enjoyed a good walk."

Orsini surrendered the note with a smirk. "You were gone all night."

"I fell asleep under a tree. I'm a fisherman, I can sleep anywhere. Besides, this room is a little stuffy. How is your room?"

"Sufficient for its needs." Orsini looked around. "I have to say your wardrobe is expensive for a fisherman."

"On loan from my brother. You went through everything?"

"I was sure you wouldn't mind. Sit, please. I wouldn't want to be accused of making anyone uncomfortable."

"I can stand."

"Can you?" Orsini had a talent for suggesting that, for half of what he said, there would be mirth down the line. "Anyway, the expensive suitcase . . ."

"My brother's. He invited me to visit."

"Are you close?"

"We're the same size, at least."

"And what a surprise to find this delightful sketch." Orsini pulled out Cenzo's portrait of Giulia from the older suitcase. "You are the artist?"

"It's nothing."

"You shouldn't be so modest. What is her name?"

"It's only for purposes of identification. She happens to be missing from home."

"Charming."

"A girl from Pellestrina."

"A fisherman's daughter? What's her name?"

"Rosa."

"Rosa what?"

"Scarpa."

"There you are. Rosa Scarpa," Orsini said. "That wasn't difficult. You must be fond of her to bring her picture all the way to Salò." Orsini held the picture close up and away. "Although I think I may detect a certain Semitic richness to her lips. How old did you say she was?"

"I don't know. Maybe fifteen."

"Let's just say a young woman. Rosa Scarpa, an extraordinary girl to have captured your imagination so." Orsini gave the sketch pad back to Cenzo. "But I'm not interested in her. I am interested in bigger fish."

What a stupid mistake to give the girl a false name and try to diminish her age, Cenzo thought. A real artist would have said the girl was a composite of many models. Now Orsini had a bone and he was going to chew it.

"Catching what?"

"Your brother, of course. I want to hear about your brother. I want to know what Giorgio Vianello is up to."

"He's a national hero."

"Maybe, but he's made you into a laughing-stock. Why are you defending him?"

"That's personal."

"What any real man would do is defend his honor. Any court would clear you, especially if I informed them of the extenuating circumstances."

"Such as?"

"Cooperation. Information about whom Giorgio sees and what he does. This war is not over. Some would have it so. There are traitors in the ranks. If I had my way, mere utterance of the word 'surrender' would be just cause for having their tongue cut out." That seemed to be a conversation stopper. Orsini's eyes were wet with emotion. He drew in a deep breath and said, "Now that I have you, things will be different."

Cenzo almost felt sorry for Giorgio. As he remembered, his brother had always been the most favored and popular of God's creatures. Men naturally gravitated to him, women flocked to him, and his political star was on the rise. Now, in the span of a few hours, two powerful enemies had invited Cenzo to murder him.

"Men like your brother must be dealt with. The time will come when the dagger is in your hand

and you must strike, but not quite yet." He sniffed the envelope for perfume. "I think your lady in the red car is waiting. Don't be late."

With the general exodus from Salò, Maria Paz had been able to choose among many villas to be the consulate of Argentina. She had found one with a veranda and flamboyant elephant-ear plants where she and a circle of friends—the film producer Otto Klein, the actress Vera Giardini, the multifaceted Giorgio Vianello—could gather in the evening and play bridge. While they played, Cenzo studied a map of Salò and Lake Garda.

"Are you all in the film business?" he asked no one in particular.

Otto Klein thoughtfully blew his nose. "You know, Cenzo, you can't swim in water without getting a little wet. It's true. We are who we are, 'playing our petty parts from day to day,' or something like that. Maria is always the lovely hostess. Vera is always an ageless ingénue."

"You brought my film?" Vera leaned toward Otto.

"Yes."

"We're having a preview," Vera whispered huskily to Cenzo. She was a blonde in flux. Today she was Lana Turner.

"No, no," Giorgio said. "He'll be bored."

Vera slapped her cards down on the table. "I hate bridge."

"Of course you do," said Giorgio. "Bridge takes sobriety, like chess."

"Chess is even worse. All you do is sit and wait," said Vera.

"Chess is antisocial," Giorgio agreed. "The last time Cenzo and I played, years ago, he threw his pieces across the room."

"Actually," Cenzo said, "you lost and threw the board across the room."

"What are you talking about?"

"Rook takes queen," Cenzo said. "I sacrificed my queen and pinned your rook. From there, it was mate in five."

"Nonsense," Giorgio said. "The man is crazy. Are we still playing this game?" He folded his cards. "I guess not. In that case, does anyone want another martini? I promise this one will be dry enough even for my brother, that well-known grandmaster from Pellestrina."

"No, thanks," Cenzo said.

"Maria?"

"Absolutely."

"Who else? Vera?"

"Please." Vera couldn't help herself.

Neither Otto nor Vera had official status; in fact, they were universally despised, Otto for smuggling gold to Spain in the diplomatic pouch, and Vera for being an actress who gave her best performances in bed. She was shallow but untouchable, because her best friend, Claretta, was Mussolini's mistress.

"How is Il Duce?" Giorgio asked.

"You know," Vera said. "Defiant one moment, depressed the next."

"Well, who wouldn't be?" Otto lit a cigarette. "You go from darling of the world one day to being measured for a rope the next, it can get you down. This is when steadfast friends are most appreciated."

"Which friends might they be?" Giorgio asked.

"We'll see who he goes running to: that fat peasant, Rachele, or our lovely Claretta," Vera said.

"Rachele is Mussolini's wife and the mother of his children," Cenzo said. "That might count for something."

Maria changed the subject. "Cenzo, are you a fighter pilot like your brother?"

"He didn't have the nerve for it," Giorgio said.

"What does that mean?" Maria asked.

"In Abyssinia I flew a reconnaissance plane," Cenzo said. "When they ordered me to drop mustard gas on the natives, I refused and haven't flown since."

"You were lucky you weren't shot for disobeying orders," Giorgio said.

"They had me digging graves."

"As long as it wasn't your own. I can tell you're a sly one." Otto sipped from his glass. "An excellent martini. I can always depend on the Lion of Tripoli."

"I knew a man who taught his pet monkey how to make a perfect martini," Maria said. "The poor animal ended up a complete dipsomaniac. Otto, you were going to show us Vera's film. A rough cut."

"I'll get it," Otto said, and bounced to his feet.

"It's not really my film," Vera said, "but it is a speaking part."

"In bed or out?" Giorgio asked.

"That's cruel," said Maria.

"Claretta saw the film and was very impressed," said Vera. "I mean, we have to bolster our spirits. We can't just lie in bed and eat chocolates."

"Isn't that what Nero did while Rome burned?" Giorgio asked. "Popped chocolates and watched movies?"

"You're heartless," Vera said.

Otto Klein staggered onto the veranda under the weight of a cardboard box stuffed with film reels. "I'm sorry, Vera. Sorry, my sweet. The film is in the can but I don't think we'll be able to distribute it in time."

"In time for what?" Vera asked.

"The end of the war, darling, the end of the war. But when the war is over we'll be first in line with a product in hand."

"Are we talking about my film?" Vera asked.

"There's a detail here and there we'll have to change. The swastikas." Klein set the box down. "Wait just a second, the projector is in the car."

He dashed out.

"It's interesting how madmen gravitate to film." Giorgio poured himself a martini. "And, of course, beautiful women. But then, we're to blame. We push them into it. We insist, 'You ought to be in pictures.' Actually, do you want to know the real reason why our friend Otto doesn't want to go back to Berlin? Because every film producer, Swiss or German, who does return is given a rifle and sent to the front line."

"I've got it." Klein returned with a movie projector. "The film runs a little long at three hours."

Klein threaded a reel of film onto the projector and found an outlet.

"Could you turn out the lights? What we'll see here is a scene of Nietzsche pondering the concept of the Superman." He flicked a switch and a countdown was projected against a garden wall: 6 . . . 5 . . . 4 . . . 3 . . . 2 . . . 1 . . . 0. On the make-do screen was a stairway with a suitcase on the landing.

"I think you have the wrong film," Giorgio said.

"Leave it," Cenzo said.

The camera established that the stairway was half in ruins and the ceiling was caved in. Footsteps climbed to the landing and a young woman in a hat and coat appeared. She turned to the camera and said, "It's here, just where I left it."

Her voice was more chirpy than Cenzo remembered, and her face positively glowed in the spotlight. But the director was not happy.

"No, Gina. No, no, no. This is a climactic moment. You can't just saunter up the stairs. This bag holds everything in the world that is important to you. When you find it, you have to clutch it to your breast. You want to squeeze tears from the audience. Do you think you can do that, sweetheart? Run up the stairs, hit your mark, turn toward the camera, and say, as if your life depended on it, 'It's here, just where I left it.'" She nodded obligingly but Cenzo could see her anxiety. The camera jiggled and dust rose. A bomb hit in the distance. "Not even close, children. Let's try again. Gina to the bottom of the stairs and . . . *Action!*"

Gina stumbled on the first step.

"My stupid feet."

"Relax. A deep breath. Everyone loves you. Go."

She ran up the stairs but, as she turned to deliver her line, drew a blank. "I'm hopeless. I'm letting everybody down."

"Nonsense, you're just nervous. Giorgio, I hate to say this, but I think having you here makes Gina a little tense. Would you mind stepping outside for ten minutes? We have to change reels anyway. Then, when we're done, we'll have some schnapps and cigarettes for the entire crew. Is that camera still running? Then—"

The screen went black and a tail of film flipped around the reel until Klein turned off the projector. "I'm sorry, everyone. I had no idea."

The rest of the party was silent. Cenzo looked for Giorgio, but Giorgio was gone.

The lakefront was busy with trucks slowly grinding at a blackout pace. Overhead, the nightly stream of bombers poured west toward Verona and Milan.

Cenzo spotted Giorgio and kept pace with him a block behind. Whether he was being followed or not did not bother Giorgio. Whether he was seen did not bother Cenzo. He pulled the Beretta from his jacket pocket.

When Gina appeared on the screen, she was so three-dimensional, he could have touched her hand. Her voice was high and echoey, but he heard it to his bones and her apology resonated with childish notes unique to her; and for a moment she was alive, as she would be if Giorgio had not played on her fantasies.

Was it a matter of greed in Giorgio, the capture of Cenzo's queen? The need to dominate? The impulse to take away his brother's wife?

Ministry buildings ran the length of the Corso. Giorgio turned to back streets shadowed by cypresses and pines. The scene offered more pathos than dignity, with Gina reduced to tears over her own poor playacting. "It's here, just where

I left it." The suitcase beckoned. Stars blinked.

Cenzo expected that after he shot Giorgio, soldiers would shoot him. Well, for once, the brothers would come out even. The overloaded trucks lumbered by. Giorgio turned and faced Cenzo.

Cenzo held the gun out until his arm began to ache.

Until Giorgio laughed and walked away.

18

Cenzo dreamt that he was a fish in shallow water and someone was trying to skewer him with a spear. There was a great thrashing and much blood and a staccato rapping of a Mustang's machine guns raking the sea. Hugo swam the wrong way, facing down to escape the bullets, but they swarmed around him like bees. Giorgio dove after and caught Hugo by the heels. No one could swim like Giorgio, but Hugo dragged him deeper as balls of quicksilver poured from his mouth. Cenzo bolted upright and awake.

Sleep was impossible. He dressed and left the Hotel Golfo to walk the same route Maria had originally taken him on. There were soldiers on every corner and antiaircraft batteries along the waterfront, but he went unchallenged by the curfew. Either he passed as his brother or there was an assumption among the Germans that they were all citizens of the night.

Socializing with Giorgio's circle of friends was like taking part in a sinister farce. How had Cenzo been sucked in? At any moment he would be unmasked. Here he was, in a mountain resort that had become the world capital of lunacy.

He heard a familiar voice. "Is that you, Cenzo?"

It was Maria Paz, speaking to him from the veranda of the Argentine consulate. She was in a state of dishabille, her hair half-brushed, her bathrobe loosely tied, a woman rather than a fashion plate.

"I was just taking a walk," he said.

"Why?"

"No good reason. I didn't realize I was back here already."

"That happens. Anyway, I'm up for the day. Come in and have a cup of coffee with me." She opened the door and led him into the consulate's reception room.

"I don't want to wake your husband."

"You couldn't wake the consul with a cannon." She turned off her desk lamp and shoved papers into a drawer. "I'm done here."

"You still call him the consul even though you have no consulate?"

"In my eyes, he still is. I hope you don't mind if we have coffee out on the veranda."

She disappeared into the kitchen and returned

176

with a tray laden with cups and saucers and a pot of coffee. He brushed dead leaves off a table so that she could set down the tray.

"You just missed Vera," she said.

"This early in the morning?"

"She never left. She has a lot on her mind and wanted to talk, although talking with Vera is not like having a real conversation."

"What do you mean?" Cenzo asked.

"She's a good soul, even if a little self-indulgent and given to fantasy. But as you can see, the population in Salò is diminishing day by day and we put up with each other."

"I take it she's a good friend of Mussolini's mistress."

"Yes, she takes advantage of Claretta's friendship, but then Claretta takes advantage of her. She needs a shoulder to cry on."

"Vera should put as much distance as she can between herself and Claretta," he said. "What did you talk about?"

"It's always the same issue: who gets to stay with Benito Mussolini and accompany him to hell." She poured the coffee. "With Mussolini's wife, it's pride. At least with Claretta, it's love."

"What about you? Why are you still here?"

"The consul can't be moved, and besides, we have unofficial diplomatic immunity."

"That works?"

"It seems to."

"You're able to carry on here?"

"There's always work during a political upheaval."

"Doing what?"

"This and that."

Cenzo looked up at a window, because for a moment he thought he saw a figure move behind the drapes.

"What about Otto Klein?" he asked.

"I see a rope and a lamppost in Otto's future."

"And Giorgio? What about him?"

"Now, there's an interesting question. I've always asked myself: Is Giorgio a Fascist, a hero, or a film star? Never discount the allure of a film star in Italy." She reached into a bathrobe pocket for her cigarette case and let him light a cigarette for her. "And now I have question for you, Cenzo: Are you a decoy? If I were you, I would take that question very seriously. Bigger mistakes have been made."

"I'm not at all like Giorgio."

"Then you haven't looked in the mirror lately."

The dawn was an overarching red. The lemons on the veranda's trees were dark, ponderous, and ugly. Again Cenzo thought he noticed movement behind the upstairs drapes.

"You know, you shouldn't fool yourself about Gina," Maria said. "She was an ordinary girl with a beautiful face. Not a good actress, I'm afraid. She didn't deserve to die in an air raid. No one does. Yet you've sacrificed yourself to her memory. I hope you don't mind me saying this. I only ask that you consider the possibility."

"That I've been a fool? Isn't that what love is: blind?"

"And now you have a new quest, this niece of yours."

"She's just a girl. Besides, she may not even be alive."

"Exactly. Next she'll be a saint." Maria put her hand out as if she could snatch the words back. "I'm sorry. I'm just a bitter woman having a coffee at the end of the world."

There was a mechanical sound from the interior of the house, the engagement of a motor, the unreeling of cable, and the opening of an elevator grate. A light went on and a shadowy figure of a man in a robe appeared at the steps of the veranda. He was gray, as if drained and wrapped in cobwebs, and he shuffled forward dragging one foot. A woman in white, apparently a nurse, supported him.

"A visitor?" he asked.

"He was just going, dear," Maria said.

He blinked. "Did I do well?"

"You did very well." She turned to Cenzo. "This is my husband, the consul general Alejandro Paz Rodriguez."

The former consul made an effort to look at Cenzo, but his energy did not extend that far. "Is the visitor going now?" he whispered.

"Yes, dear."

Maria got up to help the aide steer her husband back to the elevator. To Cenzo she said, "I know what it's like to love someone unattainable. This is the man I loved. This is the man I still love."

Cenzo said nothing. If the world was on the point of blowing up, what was there to say?

Maria picked the car keys off the table. "Give me fifteen minutes. I'll drive you back."

Without the finishing touches of makeup, Maria Paz was a blunter beauty in a jumpsuit and sandals, on the prowl in her red convertible.

"The consul was a diplomat in Buenos Aires and I was a juvenile thief. There's no point in hiding the fact now. I seduced him. It was a scandal and the end of his career. We were allowed to marry if we left the country, so we began making the rounds, serving in lesser embassies. We were a pair. Alejandro was a man of a highborn family and I was his tramp. As you can imagine, being the Argentine consul to the Republic of Salò is the bottom of the pit. The only other nations that recognize Salò are Germany and Japan. The German representative left months ago and the Japanese never did more than send a letter. So you could say that Alejandro and I are what remain of the diplomatic corps. Or I am, after his stroke."

"What sort of thief were you?" Cenzo asked.

"An accomplished one." She turned a smile on him. "A forger."

"Of?"

"Art. The Old Masters. I learned at my father's knee."

"As a girl?"

"From the age of ten. I was a loving daughter and helping him work was an education. He died in is studio surrounded by art. That was how the police discovered us. The prosecutor himself owned a Rembrandt painted by my father. I could have laughed."

"You quit for your husband's sake?"

"For good, until Otto Klein found out about my past."

"But there are no Old Masters here to copy."

"There are, only not paintings. Violins."

Daylight filled the promenade, revealing 20mm cannons the size of siege catapults and rows of sandbags.

"Violins?"

"By Gasparo da Salò. Sixteenth-century. I may have added one or two."

"Impossible."

"Not at all, once you have a credulous buyer and you don't try to make a great violin, just an old one. You start with an ordinary fiddle with real cracks and wormholes, add some dust and ash and even some repairs. The main thing is to capture the golden quality of the varnish of a true Gasparo da Salò violin."

"Will it sound like the real thing?"

"That will be up to the buyer's imagination."

"You almost sound proud."

"Like any parent."

They had reached the Hotel Golfo.

"I think you're starting to get over Gina." Maria kissed him softly. She did so slowly but he let it happen. That was the sad part. The mutual yearning. Then a car pulled alongside and Otto Klein wound down his window. "I hope I'm not interrupting anything, but I was wondering how the consul's health is these days. I think we have time for one more run in the diplomatic pouch."

"Go away, Otto," Maria said. "I'm through with all that."

"Oh, I think the consul is robust enough."

"It's blackmail."

"Between friends? And the thing about blackmail you have to learn is that it's always based on the truth. Are we agreed? And thank you, Cenzo. You should have been an actor. Your timing was perfect."

19

He wasn't sure how he felt about Maria Paz. At the start he felt there was too little explained about her and then too much, like a box that might or might not contain high explosives. Nothing in between. Maria had averted her eyes and sped away from the Hotel Golfo without a word of explanation. Otto Klein acted as if blackmail was a normal business and perhaps for him it was.

By morning, the grand exit of the Wehrmacht had begun. Italian soldiers watched with blank faces as German troops marched by. Each side grimly ignored the other, like a marriage breaking up. At German headquarters, between the hospital and the crematorium, office workers started a bonfire of files. Motorcycles raced in twos and threes but not in panic, not yet. Cenzo thought that if any race were capable of dismantling itself in an orderly fashion, it would be Germans.

Cenzo was supposed to report to Giorgio and Colonel Steiner later at the Garda Tunnel, but he had time to kill and he bought a newspaper to read at a café. The headline declared OUR GREATEST WEAPON IS IL DUCE. Well, the Germans had come up with V-2s, Cenzo thought, so it wasn't impossible that they could stick a rocket up Mussolini's ass.

He found himself focusing on the police station at the end of the block, and when he saw that the guard post in front of it was not manned, he couldn't resist strolling in, just to pull the tail of the tiger. Posters admonished the public to report rumors and denounce traitors. On a bulletin board was a list of wanted partisans; sketches of Dante and the Spaniard were prominently displayed. Fascist martyrs were draped in velvet. A police dog wheezed in a corner. A corporal with a pencil-line mustache hunched over his telephone and assured a hysterical woman on the other end of the line that the Germans were only conducting exercises and would return.

The corporal's eyes widened when he hung up the phone.

"Giorgio Vianello?"

Cenzo had not intended to fool anyone, and for a moment he was undecided, but he saw how simple it would be to assume his brother's identity. He eased into the role the way he had slipped into Giorgio's suit of alpaca wool.

The corporal saluted Cenzo and shook his hand. "This is an honor. I'm afraid the commander's not here, but I am Corporal Fini. How can I assist you?"

"I just need to look around."

"Here?"

"Yes. We're considering a film that touches on the work of the National Police."

"Now?"

"What better time and what better way to boost public morale? I should warn you that this is not definite. Other locations are being considered."

"Would you be acting in it?"

"We'll see."

"Have you been to Hollywood?"

"Of course."

"Have you met Greta Garbo?"

"Yes."

"What is she like? Personally."

"Tall."

Corporal Fini rubbed his chin. "But you prefer to act in Italian films with Italian actors."

"For the sake of verisimilitude."

"Exactly." The corporal nodded vigorously. "I myself am full of ideas of a cinematic nature. I'd love to sit down and talk to you about them."

"Sometime. Can I count on your discretion?" Cenzo asked.

"Please." The corporal screwed up his face in an effort to look trustworthy.

"This is a story about a police officer wrongly accused of abuse of power. Do you keep records of persons who die in police custody?"

"By their own hands, yes. By hanging themselves with a belt, falling out of bed, running into a wall."

"What about assaulting an officer?"

"It happens every day."

"In political cases?"

"Most of all. Intellectuals always trip themselves up." Fini put his finger by his nose. "Always too clever by half."

Cenzo took out the photo Colonel Steiner had given him showing a man with his head beaten in. "Do you remember what happened to him?"

"Who can say? He looks like a watermelon that rolled off a truck."

"Do you recognize him?"

"No."

"He would have come through in the last few weeks. A big man with red hair traveling with a boy?"

"I'm sorry, what do you need this information for?"

"It's backstory. We build one fictional character out of many."

"Interesting."

"Of course we'll need extras, depending on where we shoot."

"Now that I think about it, there was a man who generally met your description and he was with a boy."

"What did the boy look like?"

"Skinny, off the streets, maybe fifteen years old. He had a soft cap. He stood out because a resort like Salò doesn't have many street urchins. This is not Naples."

"And he was with this man?" Cenzo tapped the photograph.

"I think so. But it's hard to say."

"You had him at headquarters?"

"Yes."

"If he was here at headquarters, you have a record of his name."

"No. We eventually let him go."

"Why?"

"There was no reason to hold him. Someone said he stole a bicycle but it was all a big mistake."

"So you let him go?"

"There was a ceremony of Fascist loyalty being conducted by the Sons of the She-Wolf when the air raid siren went off. People scattered every which way. We held on to the man but the boy vanished."

Vanishing was Giulia's talent, Cenzo thought.

"When was this?"

"About ten days ago."

"Why did you hold on to the man if there was just a mistake?"

"We didn't. But Brigade Leader Orsini had some questions of his own for the guy."

"Orsini was here?"

"That's right. The last I saw of the man, he was in the leader's car." Corporal Fini took a gulp of air. "If they're talking about shooting a film here, that's a good sign, isn't it?"

"I suppose it is." Cenzo started to leave.

"Not so fast."

"What?"

"I can't let you off that easy." The corporal opened a desk drawer and brought out a camera. "My wife will have my head if she hears that I met Giorgio Vianello and didn't take a photograph. One thing. Please don't be offended, but do you do all your own stunts?"

"Of course."

"I never doubted it."

20

There were seven tunnels along the Garda Road, each wide enough to accommodate a tank; and where the tunnels opened up, they invited spectacular plunges down to the water. The road was a perfect escape route from Salò to Switzerland. Also a perfect trap.

Colonel Steiner led Cenzo and Giorgio into the shadows of the first tunnel and unscrewed a canteen of water.

"Can you believe this?" the colonel said. "I thought I would be protecting the landmarks of civilization, masterpieces by Titian and Tintoretto. Instead, here I am, preparing to detonate a mountainside."

"None of us are doing what we thought we would," Cenzo said.

"You're right," said Steiner. "If you had questioned the men on either side of the front before the war and asked them what they thought they would be doing ten years hence, not a single man would say blowing each other up."

Some soldiers unreeled red demolition lines to bundled sticks of TNT. Some carried satchels heavy with time fuses, detonator caps, igniters, and the basic hardware of crimpers, pliers, hammers, and knives. They used pickaxes to drive holes into the walls. It was warm work, and when an axe skidded and sparked, the soldiers sucked in their breath.

"They're young," Cenzo said.

"They're boys," Steiner said. "And, like boys, they will have their toys." He stepped over what appeared to be a small "headless" tank, no more than a meter long. "A radio-controlled robot for blowing up mines. Highly entertaining. The only problem is that if a tread is disabled, the robot may go in circles or, worse, return to its maker."

"Like me," Cenzo said. "I'm returning too."

"What do you mean?" Steiner asked.

"Going back to Pellestrina."

"Like hell you are," Giorgio said.

Steiner said, "You can't be serious. You have a real talent for this sort of work. Now you're thinking of quitting?"

"I wanted to find Giulia and instead I'm going in circles. I'm not a spy."

"I never thought you were. A catalyst is what you are." Steiner paused. "Listen to these incredible echoes. Like trolls at work. No, you are doing fine. You're still our best chance of finding Giulia. And this Argentinian woman with a criminal background? She should be exploited."

"Not by me." Cenzo shot a glance at Giorgio. "It's as if you're playing a game and keeping the rules to yourself."

"Minor details."

"Such as?"

The colonel measured his words. "Vittorio Silber was a businessman with international connections."

"Even after Mussolini started rounding up the Jews?"

"Silber was protected."

"Not a fool who waited and waited and ran too late?"

"Hardly. He knew what his chances were and he took them."

"To what?" Cenzo asked.

"To come out of hiding and make contact. To negotiate an end to this endless war. To make sure that these boy soldiers would not blow up themselves or anybody else. Our rocket launcher has a bad habit of spontaneously firing. Half our weapons are sabotaged. That's what comes from using slave labor."

As a Panzer tank rolled inside, it seemed to turn the entire tunnel into the barrel of a gun. The young men laying charges were encouraged, even though the Panzer was slow and clumsy, a heavy-breathing monster and no friend of narrow spaces.

"Aren't there negotiations for peace?" Cenzo asked.

"Of course," Giorgio said. "For months and each time we are betrayed. We're hoping that Giulia would recognize the man who betrayed her father, the man who is holding up negotiations."

"And you, the Lion of Tripoli, are part of it?" Cenzo asked Giorgio.

"We needed a spokesman that people would recognize," Steiner said.

"Then you don't need me."

"We do," Steiner said. "For the same reason as before: to find Giulia. You're the only person she'll trust. The question is, can we trust you? Your brother doesn't think so. He thinks you don't want to get involved."

"He's right."

"Even to save lives?"

"Whose lives?" Cenzo asked. "You told me yourself that this war is as good as over, to sit down and wait it out."

"So you won't help us anymore?" Steiner said.

"In some last-second scheme to save the world? The world is lost."

"You sanctimonious shit." Giorgio grabbed Cenzo by the sleeve. "I've been saving you all my life."

"*You've* been saving me?"

"How do you think you could pull that stunt about poison gas in Africa without being court-martialed and shot? Or running your mouth off at Nido's bar without the Blackshirts pulling you off the street and busting your head?" He put his forearm under Cenzo's chin and pushed him against the tunnel wall. "Do something for a change. Do more than complain."

Cenzo pushed back. "You mean here is my chance to help my brother the Fascist? You think you can switch sides like an actor changing costume? It may work for women. It doesn't with me."

"So it's all about Gina again. Here we are on a battlefield and all you can talk about is her and your morality. So tell me, is Maria Paz married or not?"

Cenzo found himself unhorsed, a knight knocked out of his saddle. In a second, his moral high ground was lost.

"It would be a good thing if my boys had a chance to have a life," Steiner said. "To waste their young lives now, at the end of this war, would be obscene. Not to mention the lives of all the young men on your side."

"Who is part of this scheme of yours?" Cenzo asked. "I should know that much."

The colonel said, "I can't tell you. It's better, for everyone's safety, that you don't know."

"In case I talk?"

"That's right. The only one who knew all the pieces to the puzzle was Vittorio Silber."

"Did he know General Kassel?"

"Before the war, the general was often Silber's guest at the opera, it's true."

"Let me guess. There would be someone from American intelligence involved? And a Swiss if they're meeting in Switzerland."

"Naturally."

"And there would be a respectable Italian for ballast, like a bishop or cardinal?"

"I leave that to your brother," Steiner said. "There should be an Italian spokesman, a single voice. Giorgio is well-known and respected by both sides."

"It was felt that a familiar voice would reassure people," Giorgio said.

This was getting ridiculous, Cenzo thought. Mussolini's golden boy was going to end up a winner once again.

"Partisans included?" Cenzo asked.

"Absolutely," Steiner said. "It could be the first time you and Giorgio worked together since the two of you were boys on a fishing boat."

"There were three of us once," Cenzo said. "I'll tell you what I'm willing to do. I'll keep looking for Giulia, but I won't just hand her over to you. That has to be her decision."

"You want to make us play hide-and-seek?" Giorgio said.

"No, that's fair," Steiner said. "I think she will want to help us identify the man who betrayed her father's cause. He's a war criminal."

"She knows who he is. Have you ever heard of a lawyer named DaCosta?" Cenzo asked.

"Why?"

"His name was not called out during the raid at the hospital. She thinks it's because he was the one calling out the names."

"It would be nice if Silber had left Giulia a message," Giorgio said.

It would be, Cenzo thought. But people failed to leave messages all the time. Maps went unread and confessions went unheard. Between the intention and the act, life was often a tale told to the deaf.

The drive back to Salò was hostile and silent, as if Cenzo and Giorgio were so full of bile, they dared not open their mouths.

"The phone service still works," Giorgio said when they pulled up at the Hotel Golfo. "Call me as soon as you find the girl."

"And if I don't find her?"

"If you don't find her, go back to Pellestrina. You can keep the clothes."

"I need money and a car."

"So now you're showing initiative?" said Giorgio. "Too little, too late, as usual."

When he got back to his room, Cenzo wondered about Giorgio. Did he really believe that he had protected him all through his life? He and Giorgio were at dagger points now but at one time they had been inseparable. Giorgio, being the oldest, was the natural leader. Hugo was the baby, always underfoot. Cenzo remembered the annual celebration of Saint Joseph in Pellestrina. Giorgio had climbed a greased pole and won a pig, which made him a virtual Spartacus in Cenzo's eyes.

He thought about the painting of Hugo being strafed in the lagoon. He had painted it as a *voto*, an illustration of devotion to be hung in the church. Was it an illustration of something else? The pilot's violation of the rules of war? For the hundredth time, Cenzo remembered the stormy night, its violent bolts of lightning, himself fighting waves, Giorgio trying to rescue Hugo and, floating above it all, an apparition of the Virgin. Like many fishermen, Hugo had never learned how to swim. He desperately hung on to Giorgio's leg as the older brother beat his way to the surface, although it almost seemed that Hugo was trying to pull Giorgio to the bottom. An illusion, no doubt. An unmistakable fact was that the American fighter plane was doing its best to kill all three brothers. The illusion, however, was the reason Cenzo never hung the painting and why neither his mother nor Celestina could bear the sight of it.

21

"Cole Porter said it best. 'You're the top, you're Mussolini. You're the top, you're a dry martini.'" Vera danced across the consulate's veranda and delivered a drink to Cenzo. "Wonderful news! It looks like Rachele is going, leaving the field to Claretta. Isn't that the best? Rachele wanted to be with Il Duce but he said no."

"So true love has prevailed," Cenzo said.

"You believe in true love?" Maria leveled her gaze.

"Don't answer that," Otto said. "The only place you'll find love is in the movies. Which reminds me: Where is Giorgio?" He giggled and poured himself a gin and quinine water. "It always makes me uneasy when I don't know what Giorgio is up to."

"Our Salò social set is dwindling," Vera said. "It's like friends huddling together in the path of an oncoming storm. What is going to happen to all of us?"

"As a movie star," Otto said, "and a blonde at that, you should draw a very good price. Or at least land in the lap of an American general," Otto said.

"He's just joking." Vera was embarrassed.

"He's a cynic," Maria agreed.

"I'm simply not a hypocrite," Otto said. "An honest man is always called a cynic. You think that the liberation will be like the changing of the guard at Buckingham Palace? It won't be. It will be murderers and grave robbers, a parade of the lowest forms of humanity. You deal with them or end up with your pants down."

"Not a pretty picture, any way you look at it," said Cenzo.

"Unless you have something to trade," Otto said. "Isn't that right, Maria? A smart woman knows how to compromise. By the way, how is the consul doing? The stress can't be good for him."

"He's holding together."

"It must be frustrating for him to sit in a wheelchair while other men pay court to his wife. Figuratively speaking." He turned to Cenzo. "So, what would you trade for a girl, theoretically? I agree it all depends on the girl. Physical attributes count. Virginity, of course. I think a degree of resistance would actually be a bonus of sorts."

"For some men," said Cenzo.

"I'm sure that, when it comes right down to it, Mussolini and Claretta have some sort of escape plan," Vera said.

"Do you remember Mussolini's plan for air raid alarms?" Otto asked. "Shouting. Get on your rooftop and shout, 'Air raid!' So, no, I do not have any faith in any escape plan concocted by Benito Mussolini."

Vera changed the subject. "Did you finish Dr. Goebbels's film?"

"*The Titanic*? We finished it last week, as a matter of fact," Otto said. "It's the greatest epic ever filmed. At least there will be no more amateurish advice from Dr. Goebbels. No more model ships or giant icebergs. We will never see its like again. At least from that director. Goebbels had him hanged. From now on, people will want something bright and cheery, with legs kicking and, of course, a pretty face. That's what gets the heart of a man like Giorgio racing, wouldn't you say so, Maria? I see the glitter of sequins and hear a Latin tango."

"Very amusing," Maria said.

"Only saying what everybody knows. Oh, Cenzo didn't? He does now."

Maria went for Otto, tripped over the liquor cart, fell and hit her head on the marble floor. She didn't bleed or lose consciousness, but she lost her sense of balance when she tried to stand.

"Put her head up. Or is it down?" Vera said.

"Put her to bed," Otto recommended. "We have accidents like this all the time in film. That's why we have a doctor on the set."

"I should take you to the hospital," Cenzo said.

"To a hospital where they cut off arms and legs? No, thank you."

Cenzo supported her up the stairs to a bedroom that was distinctly feminine, with lace curtains and flocked wallpaper.

He found Señor Paz in a hospital-style bedroom near the elevator at the end of the hall. The former consul lay in a stupor. On a tray next to him were empty syrettes of morphine. In a chair, the nurse had passed into her own drug-induced stupor, her white shoes tucked to the side.

Cenzo decided to let them sleep and returned to the reception room. He turned on the desk lamp and played its light over portraits of grim South American statesmen.

Little mail reached Salò, but what correspondence came through was hand-delivered and bore the stamp WEHRMACHT: TOP SECRET. Two envelopes identical and heavier than usual lay on the desk. They did not constitute much work but more than he would have expected from a consulate that was no longer functioning and a consul too sick to rise from his bed. Cenzo picked up the top letter and an Argentinian passport slid out. A stamped photo of Wilhelm Christian Doorf looked back at him. He was blond, born May 2, 1895, in Buenos Aires, Argentina. A German name was not unusual: ten percent of the Argentine population was German and ten percent was Italian. They accounted for Argentina's sympathies during the war.

An ID said that Doorf was a mining engineer residing in Tucumán, Argentina, who had been discharged from the military with a document for good behavior and was a member in good standing at the Santo Cristo Sports Club. Cenzo opened the second envelope. It was for Manuel Cristobal Reyes, a dark, heavy-set schoolteacher, born in Corrientes, January 18, 1910. Reyes carried membership in the Argentine Teachers Union and Huracán Football Club. The last Cenzo had seen of either Doorf or Reyes was in formal SS uniforms at the birthday party for Hitler.

"It's disappointing, isn't it?" Otto said as he walked in from the veranda.

"You're still here?" Cenzo asked. "I thought you had gone."

"Vera left but I decided to stay." The clock chimed with bell tones. He checked his pocket watch like a stationmaster, satisfied that his railroad was running on schedule. "Now that you have discovered Maria's side business, what do you think?"

"She seems to be a talented forger."

"Don't be shocked. Everyone compromises. It so happens that Maria needs money and these gentlemen need to travel. Their needs meet."

"Where do you fit in?" Cenzo asked.

"Oh, I'm just a middleman. I merely address the need."

"That's very Swiss of you."

"Tell me, have you found your niece?" Otto asked.

"No."

"How much time do you think you have? Let me put it another way: How long do you think the Salò government will stand after our German comrades leave? A week?"

"More or less."

"I agree. The partisans will swarm in. I tried to convince Vera of this obvious fact but she is true to her friend Claretta, who is true to Mussolini. When the Republic of Salò folds, it won't be a pretty sight. Streets will be flooded with partisans taking revenge. Worse, most of them will be communists."

"What about Vera?"

"In her defenseless way, Vera has always been able to find a protector. As one man rolls out of her bed, another one tumbles in."

"What are you going to do? Stay with Mussolini or betray him?"

"There's no one to betray," Maria said. She had come halfway down the stairway. Her hair was a little undone and she was unsteady, but her pallor was gone. "It's all an illusion now. Il Duce always was an illusionist, right from the start."

"Aren't you an illusionist too?" Cenzo asked. "Creating passports for Nazis? That's not the same as doctoring old violins."

"It's not what you think."

"What is it?"

Maria dropped her usual sardonic smile. "I don't know."

"I congratulate you," Cenzo said. "It looks like expert work."

"Maria is the best counterfeiter of passports I've ever met," Otto said. "She can turn a Berliner into a gaucho from the pampas. We're not talking about ordinary soldiers. I mean war criminals of the blackest sort who are getting out while they can. The price goes up accordingly. Quite an artist is our Maria Paz."

"Maria, do we have guests?" The consul stood at the top of the stairs, vaguely waving his arms as if brushing aside cobwebs.

She rushed up the stairs. "They were just going."

"Introduce me."

"Some other time, darling."

"What a shame. I don't see many people, you know."

Maria paused at the top of the stairs. "You know what Otto's doing, Cenzo? He's like the manager of a flea circus who enjoys seeing his little acrobats pull carts and jump through hoops. Now he's training you."

Otto replaced the passports in their envelopes and put them on the desk. "As I was saying, everybody compromises. At times like these, there is nothing ignoble about survival. Lord knows what your missing niece has had to do to survive." He let that idea fester. "If you believe the world is made of ice cream and cakes, I have nothing to offer you. But if you don't think so—if you think the world is made up of foolhardy young women and monsters that prey on them—I can help you. How can you say no?"

It was true, Cenzo had spent all his moral indignation.

"Let me teach you," Otto said.

Otto drove. He headed to tourist cabins of pre-war Salò that had been turned into bivouacs for German troops. Stately poplars gave way to rugged pines, and wind socks of an airstrip snapped in a nighttime breeze. The runway had been a golf course, and signs of this previous existence were a clubhouse and patches of sand.

Otto rubbed his hands in satisfaction when they got out of the car.

"We should learn from Il Duce," he said. "He's not such a fool. He can turn the worthless paper of the Fascist Republic into gold and steal a fortune right from under our nose."

"I thought the Fascists were bankrupt," Cenzo said.

"There's plenty of money to be made out of a bankruptcy," Otto said. "Believe me, I've done it more than once myself. Communist? Fascist? Gold bullion doesn't care about politics. Neither do Swiss marks or notes of credit. While we thought Mussolini was wandering aimlessly around Italy, he's been emptying federal cash boxes and withdrawing party funds. He's been peeling off money like banana skins."

"And you're asking me to fly that gold out?"

"Exactly."

"I haven't flown in years."

"It's a Stork, a little reconnaissance airplane. There shouldn't be any problem. Nobody owns the gold. It's free and clear. If you don't want any of it, give it to the girl. She's due for a change in luck, isn't she?"

"How about the partisans? Maybe they think it's their due."

"They would. But all we have to do is tell the

Fascists that the partisans stole it or the other way around. Or stage a crash in the water."

"What do you expect the Germans to do? Just watch?"

"The officers in charge are more concerned about war trials to come. It's not their money. By the time they know what's happening, we'll be gone."

"To where?"

"Switzerland."

"If you're Swiss, why don't you just leave?"

"I made the mistake of producing films at transit camps for the Germans. Films of happy Jews and their cultural events. There were some very talented actors and musicians among them. They were happy to dance and sing if that gained them one more day before climbing back onto the train to their final destination. I was not necessarily proud of my work. It wasn't *The Titanic*, but it was unavoidable."

"It was propaganda."

"In the film business, you take what you can get. So you see, I'm not such a bad fellow, after all. I think we will work well together."

"You think so?"

"Simply concentrate on the mission," Otto said. "After a while, you will find that as they're being processed and stripped, they no longer have faces. All they have is a sameness."

"You've studied this?"

"Naturally. A Junker bomber can carry twenty passengers and a pilot. But a Stork reconnaissance plane like you flew in Africa can lift on a breeze while a Junker needs at least four hundred meters to clear the ground. Really, there is no choice but the Stork. Wouldn't you agree?"

It was true. On such a short airstrip a Junker would stand out like an overdressed dowager.

"You won't find the girl on your own," Otto said. "You can hardly ask the Germans for help, and the partisans will be too busy taking over the world. Do you think Giorgio is going to help you, anymore than we would help him?" Otto allowed himself an expansive puff. "What you need is someone with the right contacts."

"Why would you help find her?"

"Because you can help me."

Cenzo heard the brassy sound of a small plane.

Otto looked at his watch. "Right on time." A German reconnaissance plane skimmed the treetops. Otto was grimly satisfied. "One of our German friends is leaving the battle early with the help of the Argentine consulate, of course."

The plane looked as frail as a model made of balsa and glue, but it was a Stork, the plane that had once rescued Mussolini from a mountaintop and still flew in and out of Berlin. It made a low pass over the landing strip, turned into the wind, touched down, and rolled to a gentle stop on the grass.

A car stripped of its swastikas appeared at the clubhouse, and as the passenger emerged, Cenzo recognized the obese colonel who had delivered a birthday toast to Hitler at General Kassel's farewell dinner. Tonight he was in civilian clothes and clamped a fedora on his head as he scurried to the open door of the plane. Cenzo remembered the name on his passport. Herr Wilhelm Christian Doorf.

The pilot was a young man in black leather, a tight black helmet, and a lighthearted mood, as if all he had ever wished for was a spectacular death. He walked toward Otto and said, "I have the ratline if you have the rat."

"Here are his papers, all in order." Otto passed him an envelope. "Everything in context."

The pilot riffled through the contents with an expression so blank, it had to be contempt. Otto was not put out; he looked as if he had been insulted by better men.

"Very well." The pilot turned on his heel and marched back to the plane to squeeze his passenger's wide rump into the rear seat. He climbed into the front, pulled on his helmet like a knight of yore, and started the engine. The plane nudged forward, made a 180-degree turn, and rolled into the wind. As always, the takeoff of a Stork seemed premature. One bump and the recon plane was grass-high, then high as the trees and banking toward Switzerland. The car that the colonel had come in backed up and drove away.

"Do you remember how to fly one of these toys?" Otto asked.

"They may be simple, but they're not toys."

"I didn't mean to insult you. Dodging bullets must take skill."

"Mainly, you fly close to the ground."

"I'm sure you do."

"I'll pass," Cenzo said.

"It's a good plan."

"It's not the plan that bothers me."

"You don't trust me? You can pilot the plane and the girl will hold the gun. You can't object to that."

"I'm not interested."

"Not your cup of tea? Well, think about it. You'll see, it's the only way out."

The clouds opened up and rain began to fall. Cenzo could picture the Stork being blown like a kite one way and then the other.

22

A battalion of the Wehrmacht was leaving Salò, marching down the promenade to the ringing of a glockenspiel that made their retreat sound like a celebration. Who were they? Cenzo wondered. Strip them of their helmets and guns, and they were salesclerks and students who had been dispatched to oblivion. There were salutes and cheers outside German headquarters but the locals greeted them with the impatience of hosts whose guests had overstayed their welcome.

Cenzo picked up a copy of the *Gazette*. The war was taking on strange twists and turns. Before, the Germans had advertised for sausage makers; now it was for blacksmiths. They sent them to Poland to work in arms factories, yet they continued to mount productions of grand opera and announce fictitious victories over the Allies.

Maria Paz squeezed next to Cenzo with a manila envelope under her arm. "I've been looking for you," she said.

"And now you've found me. But, no, thank you. I don't need any passports to Argentina."

"Do you despise me?"

"For helping Nazis escape a fate they richly deserve? A little."

Maria was still fashionable, always fashionable, in a creamy-white dress that brought out her natural tan. It was interesting, he thought, how initial attraction could inspire later contempt.

"You would never compromise," Maria said. "Not you."

"Since I'm just a lowly fisherman I can pick and choose. Does this music stir your blood? It's a bit oompah for my taste."

"You don't want to talk to me?" she asked.

"No. You are far too clever, both you and Otto. Why were you looking for me?"

"I thought you would like to know that Giulia is at Vera's house."

"Say that again."

"Vera has your girl Giulia. She called me to tell you."

"I'll meet you there."

"You go on ahead," Maria said. "You be Sir Galahad. That's a fate you deserve."

Vera admitted it was pure chance that the very girl Cenzo was searching for had visited Vera's Hollywood-style bungalow. "I mean, it's better than dramatic: it's cinematic. She's hungry, of course. Who isn't?" Vera pointed to a food tray of picked-over sandwiches and grapes that had been rolled to poolside. Modern art hung on the walls. A tiger skin sprawled across the floor.

"And you think this is the girl I'm after?" Cenzo said.

"She certainly fits the description."

"Where is she?" Cenzo asked.

"In the living room."

He knew from the moment he saw the girl hunched over a pile of Spam, soap, and cigarettes. She boldly raised her gaze as Cenzo approached. She had a round face with black hair short as a boy's and eyes that shone like black glass.

"She didn't need to sneak in," Vera said. "I told

her she could come and swim anytime except, of course, when I have male friends. I found plenty of nice dresses that fit her. It's the most extraordinary thing. What will happen to her?"

"It's not her," Cenzo said.

"You're sure?" Vera hated to lose a good story. "She swims like a dolphin."

"She may swim like a dolphin, but she's not Giulia."

"But she's so clever," Vera said.

"Of course she's clever. She's a Gypsy," Cenzo said. "Gypsies also have a difficult time with the Nazis."

The girl broke into a broad smile. "It doesn't matter. This was my last visit here anyway." From her sundress she pulled a handkerchief that she spread over the table before her and industriously began filling with black-market treasure.

"You're sure she's not the girl you're searching for?" Vera sounded cheated. "Then where is she?"

"Your guess is as good as mine."

"Well," said Vera, "it's one of those instances where two people seem to be exactly alike until someone says they're not and then all sorts of differences are uncovered. Like a birthmark. It happens in films all the time."

The girl built a pyramid of Spam, cigarettes, soap, and bottles of face cream and perfume on her handkerchief.

"She's really taking quite a haul," Vera said in a weak protest.

The girl told Cenzo, "Your lady friend here has a ton more. She's a hoarder. She should be ashamed."

"Why make this your last trip?" Cenzo asked the girl. "You could have tapped these people forever."

"Look around. The war is almost over. Once the partisans are in control, your friends are going to be . . ." The girl drew her finger across her neck.

"How did you learn to swim?" Cenzo asked.

"I dove for coins that tourists threw in the lake. When there were tourists. It was a good deal. I'm sorry it's over." The girl tied the four corners of the handkerchief into a knot and practically swung her legs with pleasure for hoodwinking people who were so gullible.

23

Cenzo parked across from the Argentine consulate. He didn't like how he had left her the day before. What, after all, gave him the right to judge her? She had been a friend to him and he had no good reason to be self-righteous.

There were no lights on or signs of life apart from the coolness of an oncoming storm. The leaves of an elephant-ear plant flapped on the veranda. A lemon rolled across the tiles. The front door flew open and shut without rousing anyone. Finally, Cenzo crossed the street and rang the doorbell. When no one answered, he pushed the door open and walked in. The loudest sounds in the reception room were the ticking of the clock on the mantelpiece and the stirring of the chandelier.

He had seen Maria stuff papers into the center drawer of her desk. It was locked, but the desk's side drawers yielded stationery, pens, ink, stamps, a stapler, and a flashlight. He flicked the flashlight beam around bookcases and travel posters. Hadn't Otto said it was a shame that Cenzo couldn't see more of Maria's handiwork? How many Nazis had she, with her talent for the bogus, sped on their way?

At the far end of the reception area was a sliver of light. Cenzo opened a door to a flight of cellar stairs and was hit by the sharp smell of turpentine. He followed the steps down to a workshop where Maria sat on a stool and polished a violin. The strings were yet to be attached. She gave a start at the sight of Cenzo but went on with her work. She wore an apron and had pulled her hair back into a workmanlike bun.

Forms of unfinished violins hung belly-out along the wall. Jars of spirit varnish, copal, volcano ash, ox blood, and gold lined the table. Penknives and sable brushes sat in open boxes, along with sets of chisels and gouges and sand-paper that ran from fine to superfine. A manila envelope sat on a workbench.

"People claim that Gasparo da Salò used gold and blood in the varnish," Maria said. "It's a myth, but buyers love to hear it."

"What else do you tell them?"

"I tell them the ingredients of the varnish were a secret. It's all contradiction anyway. On one Gasparo violin the scrolls are ugly. On another Gasparo the scrolls are elegant. Age is the most important part. It's not easy to find a violin that's four hundred years old and still intact whether it's good or bad. But if you're going to look for a Gasparo in a hayloft, Salò is the place."

"How will it play?" Cenzo asked.

"That depends on the player. I make no promises, only possibilities. I'm afraid the same can be said about Vera's Gypsy. I'm sorry I got your hopes up."

"It's the way of the world. In any case, *I* should be apologizing to *you*."

Maria fell silent. She ran her hand over the violin she had been working on, along the ancient wood and hints of mystery and gold.

"Do you get to play any of your violins?" Cenzo asked her.

"I used to." Maria looked at the array of musical instruments hanging on the wall. "I'm afraid I'm not going to be able to finish any of these in time. I'm sorry, because I would have loved to hear them played by a real musician." She eyed the line of the violin's belly and the bridge. "Notice how Gasparo kept the arching low, as if the instrument yearned to be handled."

"Does it?"

"Of course."

He picked up a manila envelope and shook its contents onto the table.

"It's not what you think," she said. They were like the identity documentation that Cenzo had seen before—passports of different nationalities, letters of transit, union cards, honorable discharges from the military, train tickets—except that the ultimate destination for these was Palestine. Whole families were listed.

"Jews," Cenzo said.

"Like Giulia. My coconspirators and I have an arrangement. We let one Nazi go in exchange for five to ten Jews."

"And if I had found Giulia, you would have created a passport and papers for her too?"

"*If* you had found her," Giorgio said from the top of the stairs. He stepped down. "Why is he here?"

"That's what I was going to ask you," said Maria. "I expected you. That's why I left the doors unlocked."

Cenzo felt very much on the wrong foot, as if he had arrived at a party on the wrong day.

"What do you think?" Giorgio asked Maria Paz. "Is he dangerous?"

She gave Cenzo a cool assessment. "I don't think so."

"You'd be surprised," Giorgio said. "Can you believe, Cenzo actually passed himself off as me at police headquarters? Now, that's ambition."

"I don't think so," Cenzo said.

"It doesn't matter. We're running out of time."

"I'm almost finished with the passports," Maria said.

"You've got to get ready to meet the conquering Allies. I've just heard on the radio that Argentina has declared war on Germany and Salò too."

"That should tip the scales," Maria said. "Argentina against Salò. Could a war be any more ridiculous?"

"I'll have to get back to the radio station," Giorgio said.

"To be the voice that announces the surrender, of course," Cenzo said.

"Once things start to fall apart, it will be too late," Giorgio said to Maria. "Come to the station with me."

"They can't be that close," Maria said.

"On some streets, partisans are here already."

"I can't leave the consul."

"The object now is to avoid chaos. Somebody has to have control of the radio, the railroad, the armory, the streets."

"And the partisans?" Cenzo asked.

"The Reds, you mean. They have to be neutralized. That's why the right people have to be in charge when the Allies come marching in."

24

Rumor had it that Mussolini was hiding with the cardinal in Milan. That loyal Fascists were rallying by the thousands to his banner. That he was going into retirement to write his memoirs. That Germans and Allies were joining forces to attack communist Russia. None of these stories were true. But it was the eve of something enormous, a collective breath held, a sense that a great wave was on the horizon.

The only model of equanimity that Cenzo encountered was Otto Klein, who walked along the Corso like a man appraising real estate.

"I always leave room for compromise," he said. "Sober-headed businessmen can always work something out." That seemed to be the case with Otto Klein.

"If you get fair warning," Cenzo said.

"Of course I'll get fair warning. There are alarms and false alarms. I have my dear friend Vera, who will get her signal to leave from Claretta, who will get her signal from Mussolini. It's probably the only system in Italy that works. Where are you headed, Cenzo, if I might ask?"

"To the cathedral."

"I wouldn't have figured you as a religious type." From time to time, Otto skipped to keep pace. "Meeting anyone I know?"

"My brother. You know, Otto, you make me feel like I'm being squeezed for plumpness."

"Nonsense."

The cathedral trembled as a Panzer tank rolled by. Negotiating a turn, the tank clipped a kiosk and dragged it like a hostage down the street. Otto framed the scene with his fingers.

"I can't help myself, I'm a moviemaker. Imagine what it will look like when the enemy enters Venice. How epic it will be. The last stand of civilization against a horde of American mobsters, the dregs of the British Empire, perverts of the French Empire, lascivious Africans and mercenary Sikhs."

"For a peace-loving Swiss, you have a blood-thirsty appetite," Cenzo said. "What if the Germans simply leave quietly?"

"Not their style."

The Cathedral of Salò was so narrow it seemed pinched. Worshippers floated in the watery illumination of candles, and it took Cenzo a minute to find Giorgio. A crucifix hung in the light that poured in from a window high above the altar.

Giorgio whispered, "The cathedral is on the site of a Roman temple. I like to imagine Bacchus rising from the floor. Crucifixes are usually so dismal, but if you disregard the wormholes, this one has a certain elegance."

Cenzo took in the worshippers. A man who looked flattened by life wore a mourning band on his sleeve. A nun mumbled to her rosary. Two girls whispered secrets to each other. A fat man gathered his arms like an octopus. A program from Vatican Radio whispered by the front portal. A swallow circled the transept.

"What do you want?" Cenzo asked.

"Have you found your friend?" Giorgio asked.

"No."

"Then what have you been doing, besides poking your nose into the affairs of Maria Paz?"

"Your nose is already there."

"That's crude. I should have left you back in Pellestrina."

"You would have. It was Steiner who wanted me," said Cenzo.

"Colonel Steiner? You think he cares about Giulia—or any Jew, for that matter? He just wants to end the war while the German army is still intact. One traitor sealed Vittorio Silber's fate and Giulia is the only one who might know who that is."

"Silber's cell was raided. Were there any others?" Cenzo asked.

"If there were, you would be the last person I would tell," Giorgio said. "We're getting off track."

"What is 'on track' according to you?" Cenzo asked.

"I want you to leave Maria Paz alone. She is busy enough taking care of the consul without dealing with you."

The swallow circled the dome, and again Cenzo thought of Hugo. In Cenzo's painting Hugo had hold of Giorgio's foot and swam downward, apparently to escape being machine-gunned by the plane. But perhaps interpretation was in the eye of the beholder. Perhaps the truth had always been evident but unacceptable. Perhaps Hugo had deliberately been swimming down and taking Giorgio with him.

But Hugo was the sweetest of the brothers. Why would he want to drown Giorgio and himself? As Nido would say, there was no reason unless there was a reason.

"Leave Maria Paz alone?" Cenzo asked. "Did you leave Celestina alone?"

"What are you saying?"

"Did you ever find yourself alone with Celestina in our mother's house? Celestina worshipped you. So did Hugo."

"What are you talking about?"

"What goes on at home when a fisherman is at sea."

"I think you're insane."

"Maybe I'm just seeing clearly. Did you cuckold both of your brothers?"

"This is outrageous. I try to help you and this is what I get."

"You think like Mussolini that you can have any woman you want."

"Did you say this to Maria?"

"It only occurred to me now." Cenzo turned to face Giorgio. "Why are you finding it so hard to say no? If I'm wrong, say so."

Giorgio stood. "I have to get back to Radio Salò. Otherwise, I would fill your mouth with your teeth."

"You can try."

Whatever Giorgio was going to say was overwhelmed by sirens that shook the crucifix where it hung. A sexton darted in the church doors and shouted, "Venice is being bombed! Those bastards. They finally did it!"

Giorgio gave Cenzo a gesture of disgust and hurried out the side door.

Cenzo pushed his way from the church into the piazza. People heard gossip and exaggerated it. St. Mark's Cathedral was in flames, the square filled with casualties, the Grand Canal choked with sunken barges, gondolas, and fireboats. It was like the Rape of the Sabines, the Sack of Rome. Great monuments of civilization were going up in flames.

25

There had been no actual bombing of Venice, no casualties and no razing of civilization to the ground, but rather a raid on the docks carried out with such precision by the RAF that, while ships were sunk, the city was spared. The largest naval target was a German gunboat that had been towed from the lagoon; it didn't have enough fuel to leave port anyway.

Cenzo was spinning from lack of direction. Let the world seek Mussolini; he sought only Giulia. If she was in Salò, would she stay or try to get back to Venice? She might follow her father's advice and meet the advancing American army. Or had DaCosta, the man who betrayed her father, caught up with her? Was she even alive?

He turned when he heard his name called out across the piazza and saw Maria's Alfa Romeo. But there was no sign of Maria. Vera was at the driver's wheel, teary and distraught. Her mouth was dark with lipstick, her blond hair was loose, and the fur of a dead fox was wrapped around her neck. The fox had beady eyes that stared at Cenzo and teeth that looked ready to snap.

"I can't get Claretta to change her mind. She insists on going with him."

Cenzo did not have to ask who "he" was.

"Going where?"

"That's it. Nowhere. He says 'Good-bye' to everybody and then he doesn't go. Or he goes to Milan and talks to the archbishop. Everyone assumes it's to surrender, but nothing happens. On the way back his car is strafed and men are killed. No matter. He's like a sleepwalker. Now Venice is attacked and where is he? Going back and forth between Claretta and Rachele. Again. When will he make up his mind?"

Probably never, he thought. "Why are you driving Maria's car?"

"She gave it to me. She said she wouldn't need it."

"Why not?"

"Something about diplomatic immunity."

"She doesn't have it. Her husband is no longer a consul."

"Well, that's what she told me. She was busy with passports. She said the Alfa Romeo would be good to barter with when the Americans came into town. I won't need it either. I'll be with Claretta and Il Duce."

"If I were you, I would settle for keeping your head. Any friend of Mussolini will not be treated gently."

"But I'm only Claretta's friend."

"Tell that to the Committee of Liberation."

Vera winced. "Do you think they're watching now?"

"They've been watching for years."

"They wouldn't hold anything against me. I'm a civilian. I never hurt anyone."

It was true. What had she done besides commiserate with her best friend, Claretta, and ease the homesickness of a few German officers? It wasn't even as if Germany was an enemy at the start. Vera happened to be in the wrong place when the tide went out.

"What about Otto?" Cenzo asked.

"I hate to say this about such a dear friend. I don't trust him."

"I know the feeling. Good luck."

Vera kissed him as if they were friends parting for the last time.

Outside the Garda Road Tunnel, Colonel Steiner and his demolition team had not heard about the RAF raid on Venice.

"Radio reception in the tunnels is miserable," the colonel said. "We can barely receive Wehrmacht orders, let alone broadcasts from the Vatican. Dare I ask, is there anything left of St. Mark's or the Grand Canal?"

"Nothing has been touched," Cenzo said.

"The Campanile?" Steiner asked. "Arsenale? Salute?"

"Not a scratch."

"So the Allies did not lay waste to the most beautiful city in the world."

"Oddly enough."

Steiner's troops followed the conversation from a distance. They were, as Steiner had said, a mix of veterans and boys. As a safety precaution no smoking was allowed. Orange flags marked the placement of antipersonnel mines, green flags marked antitank mines. The network of wires and high explosives that they had laid in the entrance of the tunnel appeared to be as elaborate as a spider's web, and intact. Cenzo recognized land mines and barrel bombs sitting on trip wires.

"There was practically no opposition in the air," Cenzo said. "With these last ships sunk, there's no movement of cargo or ammunition. The war would be over now if someone would just say so."

"It's not so simple. We were closer to surrender a month ago. Then we were organized. Now we're desperate."

"Who's 'we'?" asked Cenzo.

"A group," said Steiner. "Officers, businessmen, acceptable politicians."

"Including Giorgio?"

"Including a well-known patriot like Giorgio, yes. He always managed to keep Mussolini at arm's distance. You may not like him but other people do."

"And a respected Jew who could come out of hiding to vouch for the group."

"Vittorio Silber, yes. At least he tried. There's

no more delicate military operation than a surrender. All you need to turn a surrender into a slaughter is take away trust."

Cenzo tried to ask without insinuation, "How did you survive?"

"I'm not sure I have. I'm not an incompetent officer. If the Allies do try to force their way through the tunnels, my boys and I can mount a fair defense. We have a lake on one side and mountains on the other and tons of explosives in between. Once I've kept the peace, however, there's no more need for me."

"What makes you think the Americans would come this way at all?"

Steiner motioned Cenzo to follow and led him to a field where a car was standing among the oleanders. The backseat was covered by a tarpaulin. Steiner lifted it and raised a lantern so that Cenzo could better see a dead man in an American uniform and a knit cap. He showed no sign of a wound; it was if he had simply gone to sleep.

"An American scout. He fell from up there and broke his neck." Steiner pointed to the cliffs above the tunnel. "Just a boy. I doubt he'd ever fired a shot. He is the first raindrop of the storm to come." The colonel let the tarpaulin drop.

"And where will you be when the real fighting begins?"

"Where a professional soldier always is: between

the hammer and the anvil." Steiner rethought the proposition. "It's said that Napoleon's retreat from Russia was a disaster because his army tried to carry home too much loot. They wouldn't give up this candelabra or that set of silver. At least no one will be able to say that about us."

As he drove back to Salò, it seemed to Cenzo that time sped up and the German soldiers he passed all moved at a half trot. Clerks carrying records from German headquarters at the Grand Hotel tripped and fell, letting loose a flock of white paper. The military crematorium for limbs shut down and smoldered in its own wispy smoke.

Giorgio had made it in to Radio Salò. He advised listeners to remain calm and stay at home. He then played classical music, the usual accompaniment to disaster.

Cenzo caught only a glimpse of Il Duce's cars as a glint in the twilight. Mussolini's convoy rolled from Lake Garda to Lake Como. From there they would drive to Lake Maggiori and Lake Orto. At the start of the day rumor had it that legions of Blackshirts were massed at the Swiss border waiting for a signal from their leader. Stories dissolved into the mist. With every passing hour, Mussolini was defiant, he was abject, he was philosophical. Finally, it was said, he abandoned his wife for Claretta, who brought along her best friend, Vera.

· · ·

There were occasional gunshots, the sound of old scores being settled and small-time looting, but nothing seemed amiss at the Argentine consulate. Cenzo found Maria Paz on her veranda flat out on a chaise longue, transported so far beyond inebriated, she seemed weightless. When she steered a whisky to him, the drink cart clattered, yet she poured him a glass and didn't spill a drop.

"So," she said.

He settled in a chair. "So?"

"So why aren't you leaving like everyone else? Don't tell me. There's always a good reason," she said.

"I'm sure there is."

"But you're not sure what it is, are you?"

"No."

"That's good. That's more like the man I first met. Giorgio was actually proud that you passed yourself off as him."

Maria was a sensual display. Her color was red from her red dress to her red lipstick to her red nails. She opened another bottle of scotch.

"What shall we celebrate?" she asked.

"That the right side won."

"How can an Italian even talk about the right side?"

"Very carefully." He refilled the glasses. "Why did you give your car to Vera?"

"I'm not going anywhere. Besides, I can't afford the petrol."

"So it's practical consideration?"

"That's all," she said.

"Did you finish your passports?"

"Yes, thank God."

"How did that make you feel, having their fate in your hands? Giving Nazis the stamp of approval?"

"I saved many more Jews than Germans."

"Did the consul know what you were up to?"

"No. For Don Rodriguez, food and medicine magically appear."

"And morphine?"

"Morphine he needs most of all. Giorgio gets that from his German connections. Giorgio is a miracle worker. We owe him everything."

"Are you in love with him?"

Maria took a second. "That's a complicated question."

Cenzo remembered the breezy first day when Maria drove him around Salò. Her casual waves and kisses to the troops, even if they were German.

Maria took out a silver cigarette lighter with a Japanese willow pattern embossed on the front. Cenzo took the lighter away as she leaned forward.

"Did Giorgio give this lighter to you?"

"Yes."

"Did he show you how to use it?" He flipped open the lighter and revealed a barrel and trigger good for one bullet.

"I wouldn't have shot you."

"I didn't think you would. Does Giorgio love you?"

"Probably not."

"Do you think he loved Gina?"

"She was a onetime affair, a beautiful girl, nothing more."

"You don't think the fact that she was his brother's wife added a certain twist?"

"We've been all through this. It was pure chance you were brothers."

"Actually, there were three Vianello brothers," said Cenzo. "You can see us on the sail of our boat, *putti di mare.* Giorgio was the oldest, I was in the middle, and the youngest was Hugo. We were attacked by an Allied fighter plane. I did a painting of it. I am on deck, bleeding and praying to the Virgin, and Giorgio is in the water trying to save Hugo. The problem is I never prayed to the Virgin and Hugo and Giorgio were reversed. It wasn't Giorgio trying to save Hugo, it was Hugo trying to drown Giorgio and himself. You have to ask yourself: Why would Hugo do that? He idolized Giorgio. We both did. So did my wife, Gina, and Hugo's wife, Celestina, who is a pretty enough girl. Totally smitten around a film star. Why would Hugo do that?"

She resisted the insinuation, as Cenzo knew she would. She would turn and twist like an eel to deny a second betrayal. "Do you have a copy of this painting?" she asked. "Do you have sworn statements by the police? A photograph of the body? The death was caused by enemy gunfire. What proof do you need?"

"I'm trying to explain why a young fisherman would try to drown himself and his hero."

"Why are you telling me all this?"

"So you will know what was happening on that boat. It was a propaganda event and you know how important that is. Otherwise we would not have gone out in such foul weather. The photographers wanted pictures of Giorgio with his family and he was supposed to play a sailor home on leave who was helping his brothers in the family trade. I knew from the start there would be trouble. Both Giorgio and Hugo barely said a word, and rather than staying near the dock, where the cameramen were, Hugo sailed to the deepest water he could find. He didn't even pretend to fish.

"Then the Mustang came out of the sky. I don't know what the pilot thought he was doing— maybe getting target practice. There was nothing to be gained by strafing a fishing boat. He made two runs and went on his way. I doubt the pilot even reported seeing us. Anyway, I was on deck and Giorgio and Hugo were in the water in a cloud of blood. When I dived in to help, I saw that Hugo was trying to pull Giorgio down. I thought he had to be disoriented. It happens in flying all the time. I didn't believe my eyes and then there was too much blood for me to see. But why would Hugo do it?"

"You tell me," Maria said.

"Because Hugo loved Celestina like I loved Gina. The idea that Giorgio had seduced Celestina casually, simply because she was willing and available, was more than Hugo could bear."

He saw it in her eyes, a reflection of men struggling in the water. There you have it, Cenzo thought, an eel neatly speared.

26

Cenzo drove back to his hotel as spent as a racehorse staggering through mud, and he didn't have the energy to be outraged at finding the Black Brigade leader Orsini in his room again. There was something gruesomely intimate about Orsini's visits.

"Can you smell it?" Orsini asked. "Pigs. This area is famous for its ham."

"I know."

"The farmers let their pigs run free. They're highly intelligent animals, you know. The world isn't all fish." Was that why the brigade leader was visiting? Cenzo wondered. This piece of gustatory information?

"I suppose they lead happy lives," he said.

"Up to the butcher's block, yes, like you. I could arrest you now," Orsini said. "Arrest you or worse. In the meantime, I give you every possible way out. Your boat, the *Fatima*, was the only fishing boat in that area of the lagoon that night. You had an encounter with a German officer of the SS. Now you're alive and he is not."

"I don't know what you're talking about."

"Let me remind you that the war is not over."

"If you say so."

"Don't worry. From what I hear, Hoff will be missed by no one. Frankly, I find the Germans are overrated. They call us quitters. Who's quitting now? We could go to the Alps and hold out for ten years. Il Duce himself told me so."

Cenzo said, "If you want to help me, you can tell me what happened to my friend Eusebio Russo. I'm told you had him in your car outside police headquarters."

Orsini frowned. "Russo?"

"The fishmonger. There was some confusion about a stolen bicycle."

"Oh, I let him go. He had just fallen in with bad company and I believe in giving a man a second chance."

"A gift, of sorts?"

"You could say so."

"You wouldn't know where Russo is now?" Cenzo asked.

"I can't keep track of every criminal wandering the streets."

Then what was the source of such a gruesome photograph? Cenzo wondered. Steiner might have lied simply to enlist Cenzo's help in finding Giulia.

"Vianello, did I ever tell you what I did before the war?"

"No."

"I was a professor of entomology at the University of Bologna. My specialty was parasites."

"That must have kept you busy."

"Are you familiar with the hairworm?"

"I can't say that I am."

"Well, it's a very thin worm, obviously. Also called a grasshopper worm, although it's neither an insect nor a worm. It's a real psychological study."

"A psychological worm?"

"The hairworm larva lives in a body of water that a grasshopper happens to drink from and thus is swallowed. Then the worm grows until it fills the grasshopper's body cavity. Here the psychosis takes over. The mature worm controls the brain of the grasshopper and sends it on a suicidal search for water. As soon as the grasshopper finds it, it jumps in and drowns, allowing the worm to squirm out and complete the cycle. Now, you have to ask yourself: What was going on in the grasshopper's brain? What compelled it to take its own life? Was it fever or was it bliss?" He picked a sketch of Giulia from the top of the bureau. "What is it about this girl, Giulia, that has infected your brain? I ask because you've gone to such great lengths to find her."

"It seems to me as if people are going to great lengths to kill her."

"It depends on your point of view. Thanks to your brother, you seem to be mixing with the social elite of Salò. The former Argentinian consul general, filmmakers, General Kassel himself. Not to mention the social parasites Otto Klein and Vera Giardini. No? Too bad. There are also thousands of Fascists who have been purified by the fire of war, true patriots willing to sacrifice their all and who trust in the Fascist credo: 'Believe! Obey! Fight!'"

"I'm afraid you have the wrong man."

"Or a man desperate enough to put a gun to his brother's head. Someone who has been cuckolded and betrayed. I'd say you were a perfect fit."

"I won't help you."

"Too bad. I'm certainly prepared to help make a hero out of you." Orsini stood to go. "Well, I tried," he said. His foot shot out and squashed a cockroach that ventured from under the bed. "Filthy bug."

27

As soon as Orsini left, Cenzo dropped into bed, too tired to remove his clothes. He closed his eyes but something nagged at him, perhaps a hairworm, perhaps a pig. He remembered how many times his friend Eusebio Russo had smuggled items on the black market, in particular hams from pigs that his mother, the widow Margherita Russo, had bred and butchered. Margherita was a one-woman farm. She had a powerful personality and was "hard and broad across the beam," as she liked to say. But she lived her own life and cursed equally any Fascists or partisans who tried to steal pigs from her farm. She hid her pigs and even trained them to come at her whistle. "Pigs are smart," she would say. "Smarter than some people."

He closed his eyes and tried to sleep but he had the feeling that a hook and bait had been dragged before him. He slept fitfully for an hour, then rose from his bed like a zombie. The possibility that Russo was alive kept Cenzo's eyes wide-open.

He still had the key to Maria's Alfa Romeo, a quarter tank of petrol, and an obliging moon that lit the way inland to Brescia. Cenzo passed unchallenged by muddy soldiers and German antiaircraft batteries that huddled under camouflage nets. He had only been to the Russo farm once, but he followed his low beams for half an hour before he turned onto a dirt road that wound up the mountain. He slammed on his brakes to avoid a black hog that sat in the middle of the road.

The hog was five hundred pounds and disinclined to move. Other pigs trotted down the road along a steel fence. Cenzo thought they must have escaped and had missed a feeding—which, considering the nature of hogs, was a serious matter. Cenzo skirted the hog and drove through an open gate. Hog eyes followed him in.

"Never sleep on the ground," Signora Russo used to tell Cenzo when he visited with Eusebio. She advised him never to treat a pig like a pet unless he intended it to become a member of the family. Otherwise, to slaughter one would be like murder, with all its screaming and disbelief. Many farmers couldn't kill their own pigs. That is, if they were dealing with a friendly pig. "Otherwise, they were up against a quarter ton of angry, half-wild animal."

The Russo farm was composed of a house, barn, wet and dry wallows, troughs with dividers to keep arguments to a minimum, a yard and pen with enough space for hogs not to crush piglets, plus processing rooms and a compost pit. The pigs spent all their lives within the bounds of a farm where they became giants and were ultimately transformed into prosciutto, salami, sausage, salt bacon, lard, and chops. Signora Russo owned a truck and trailer and a Citroën 2CV automobile that looked like pleated paper. For protection, she had a pair of Alsatian guard dogs. Usually the dogs came racing up, barking and snarling as if they were going to tear apart the sky. Now they lay still on the ground.

The door to the house was open. Inside, Margherita had chosen mahogany furniture so dark it was nearly invisible. The walls were decorated with photographs of prize pigs wearing smiles of simpering goodwill. The air, however, was tainted with the smell of blood. Cenzo didn't see any yet, but he started inhaling in shallow breaths.

Eusebio Russo lay dead on the kitchen floor, one hole in his head and two in his chest. His ginger hair fanned out and his blue eyes held a glassy stare. A gun lay by his side. He was lukewarm, probably dead for hours.

Signora Margherita Russo had been shot in her bedroom. A white nightgown with lace tatting was laid out on her bed. Someone with a steady hand had shot her between the eyes. What was the sequence there? Cenzo wondered. Had Eusebio come to the house and found his mother already dead, or had Margherita heard the shot from the living room as she was preparing for bed?

In the living room a gramophone had gone silent

with a needle in the groove. The only illumination was a lantern's guttering flame.

Pigs followed Cenzo and the lantern into the barn. They vied for position over sacks of corn, grunting and snorting and pushing each other out of the way. Two pigs collided and toppled bales of hay, revealing loose boards. A massive boar spread out over the boards and seemed determined not to move. When Cenzo fired his pistol for attention, the hog stood and grudgingly backed away. Straw swirled in the light of the lantern. He moved the floorboards aside, Guilia looked up out of the dark, and he lifted her up.

"Why did you take so long? Why did you take so long? Why did you take so long??" she whispered into his ear.

"He's dead. And his mother."

"Did you see *him?*" she asked.

"Who?"

"DaCosta. He's here."

"Whoever was here, he's gone." Cenzo carried her out of the barn.

Cenzo dug shallow graves for Eusebio and Margherita, shooing the pigs away with his shovel. With their round backs, the pigs made a natural cortege.

28

By the time they returned to Salò, night had become a gray morning streaked with rain. Cenzo knew he couldn't go back to the Hotel Golfo or anywhere near Orsini's grasp. Vera had decamped to join Claretta and Mussolini and, in despair, had left her house open. Cenzo carried Giulia in.

She was still shaking. Without a word, Cenzo showered and washed her until the last grain of dirt was off her body and then toweled her off until she was smooth as marble.

What was he after? the fisherman was asked. Diamonds? Pearls? A crown of gold? Better yet, was there one dazzling insight that a man could steer his boat by? Yes. "There's plenty of fish in the sea." That was it, the wisdom of the ages. If a man could be satisfied with that grain of knowledge, he could be satisfied for life.

"Plenty of fish?" Yet only one woman would do. And not just any one, but the most obstinate, impossible woman he had ever met.

He wrapped her in his arms until her shaking died and then he brought her back to life with a kiss.

They slept into the afternoon. When Giulia awoke she found Cenzo lying on his side and looking at her. She pulled up the sheet.

"What are you staring at?"

"Colors."

"What is there to see?"

"Don't tease."

"I'm not teasing. You've been hidden too long. You don't see the way your black hair fans across your snow-white cheek." He ran his finger over her lips. "And how red and plush your lips are. In short, you have no idea how beautiful you are."

He was aware that his words were insufficient. Byron might have dashed off some poetic descriptions as if they were child's play and with a sketch pad a master like Titian would have done her justice. In bed, close enough to feel the heat of her, Cenzo was overwhelmed.

"Not thin?" she asked.

He pulled the sheet back. "Not a bit. I would say you are richly assembled."

"There ought to be a prize for that."

"I think there is."

She sucked in her breath as he unfolded her. She seemed poised, absolutely still like a small bird ready to fly. Then she guided him in and the taste of her skin was salt.

Distant gunshots finally roused them out of bed. They were ravenous and Cenzo found stale bread, hard parmesan, and unopened bottles of cheap wine for their breakfast.

"Are we safe?" Giulia asked.

"Relatively. This isn't like Naples or Rome. Once the Germans leave, Salò will be empty."

"How can you be sure?"

"This won't be a fight between Italians and Germans—it will be between Italian partisans and Italian Fascists."

"Wasn't Eusebio a partisan?"

"Eusebio was independent. He sometimes squirmed out of tight spaces by seeming to cooperate with the Germans, sometimes with the partisans, but never with the Black Brigade. He had his standards."

"He saved my life. Twice."

"Tell me what happened from the time you left with Russo. Start with the second oarsman. It's a long crossing between Pellestrina and Venice, so I understand why Eusebio wanted another oar in the water. But I was surprised to see another man in his boat."

"It was so strange. I couldn't see his face. Our faces were covered with black scarves and it was night. It was like a funeral."

"Did he say anything?"

"No. But there was a moment in the middle of the lagoon when he stopped rowing. It was odd, us in our black boat and black scarves as if we didn't exist. Then three rays appeared underneath the boat. They were luminous. You know how rays fly underwater?"

"I know."

"They stayed with us for almost a minute. Eusebio prayed the whole time. Was he religious?" she asked Cenzo.

"No, but he was profoundly superstitious."

"Then Eusebio said, 'The deal is off.' They were the only words he said. It's funny: up to that point, I had been afraid. From then on, I wasn't."

"The other man, he made you nervous?"

"Yes."

"Do you think he could have been DaCosta?" Cenzo asked.

"I don't know. Maybe. He hardly said a word, but I didn't know DaCosta so much by his voice as by his presence. I didn't see him but I felt him. Does that make sense to you?"

"Complete sense. Where did you dock in Venice?"

"The gondola yard at San Trovaso. Then we split up," Giulia said. "Eusebio and I went in one direction and the second man in another. The man was upset, I could tell that much."

"You must have seen him. He must have taken off his scarf."

"No. He rushed off and didn't even say goodbye. I asked Eusebio where we were headed and he said that, in the old days, it would have been the Bridge of Sighs, because that's where they used to bring bodies to be identified. You know Eusebio's sense of humor. He paced for a while, then took me to the train station."

"To meet someone?"

"No. He didn't meet anybody."

Perhaps Eusebio's connection at the station was late, Cenzo thought, or perhaps Russo had not expected Giulia to make it to Venice at all. He could have regarded the spectral appearance of the rays as a form of divine intervention. "Then we boarded a local train and hid out at the pig farm with his mother. I think she hoped that Eusebio and I were eloping. I stayed with them and helped out on the farm."

"I wish I'd seen that."

"He disappeared for a while on business, or so he said. She rattled on about what a fine prospect he was and how she would pray for us. Us and the pigs. We ate nothing but truffles and ham. 'Like millionaires,' the old lady said. She looked ferocious but she was actually nice, and if anyone asked, I was Giulia Vianello from the fishing village of Pellestrina. If they doubted me I could mend a net to prove it. Then Eusebio returned. He was going to take me back to Salò Cathedral for a blessing of the bicycles. I would slip into the cathedral. We would be hiding under their nose. Clever?"

Complicated, Cenzo thought. It wasn't just a matter of hiding a Jewish girl, it was a case of protecting her from an enemy who had betrayed her father.

"But an air raid siren went off and everyone ran. I saw Eusebio being stuffed into the backseat of a black Fiat. He gave me a look through the rear window and I rode away on the bike as fast as I could."

"Who was arresting him?"

"The Black Brigade. I followed the car at a distance until they took him to the brigade's headquarters. I waited outside all day until they let him go and then, once he had walked far enough away, I joined him."

"Then Eusebio took you back to his mother's farm?"

"Yes. This time he made sure there was a hiding place for me. When he heard DaCosta's car approaching, he hid me in the barn—in a hole under loose boards. Once he stacked hay bales on it, I was hidden but I was also trapped. Later, I heard gunshots, then the door to the barn was opened and DaCosta let the pigs out. He called my name just like at the hospital."

"Are you sure it was just DaCosta?"

She nodded.

"How many shots did you hear?"

"Four or five."

Cenzo was surprised. Eusebio would not have hesitated to use a gun, and his mother was no shrinking violet when it came to self-defense, yet they had been outgunned.

"How long were you in the hole?"

"Hours. I closed my eyes and hypnotized myself. You know what I thought about? Fish."

"You were on the *Fatima* too long."

"I could have stayed longer."

Why the period on the *Fatima* seemed a happy time for both of them was a mystery to Cenzo. As he remembered, all he and Giulia had done was argue.

"Tell me more about DaCosta," Cenzo said. "Did he say anything else?"

"No."

It occurred to Cenzo that he had never seen DaCosta, and searching for him was like fishing for octopus. You couldn't see it until it blinked. What would make a creature like DaCosta blink?

29

Cenzo sat in a chair with a gun in his lap while Giulia slept in Vera's bed. Her capacity for sleep was astonishing; she curled up like a cocoon while he waited for jackboots to pound up the stairs.

On the radio, between endless Beethoven and Wagner, the voice of Giorgio Vianello announced to the public, "Stay inside. Report looting. Avoid panic." Good advice, although Cenzo had to laugh at the idea of Giorgio Vianello as the voice of reason.

He heard the slap of a tailgate and moved to a window, where in the dark and the rain he witnessed a betrayal like the kiss of Judas. German SS officers lined up their Italian counterparts, took their handguns and rifles, and dragged the men to trucks. Officers of the Italian SS were outraged and confused, demanding that phone calls be placed to Hitler himself. The German SS had been their erstwhile colleagues and teachers. This was a mistake. There had to be a mistake. The fact was that the Germans were disarming them and sending them to work camps. The Italians had thrown their lot in with the wrong master and an interesting future lay ahead for them. Trained in the techniques of crowd control and interrogation, they knew all too well what to expect.

Cenzo shook Giulia awake. "We have to leave. The Germans are rounding up the Italian SS."

"That's not us."

"Not yet. But you don't have papers. I think we have to go."

"Where?"

"I have a friend at the Argentine consulate."

"How would a fisherman from the Lido know people at the Argentine consulate?" Giulia asked.

"My brother introduced me."

"That's a recommendation?"

"It's a last resort."

As soon as they were dressed, they emerged from Vera's bungalow and walked stiffly behind trucks idling in blue smoke. The street was wet and glistening from the night's rain.

"You!" a German SS sergeant prodded Cenzo with a pistol and pushed him toward a truck. "Get in!"

"What's the matter?" Giulia asked.

"Nothing, I'll take care of it," Cenzo said. "Sergeant, I am not with the SS. I am the actor Vianello."

"Into the truck."

"I broadcast for Radio Salò."

"I don't listen to that shit."

"I'm in films."

"I don't watch that shit. Get into the truck or I'll shoot your fucking foot off and we'll see how you work hopping on one foot."

Cenzo reassessed the situation. The sergeant was plainly a man with a short fuse. On the other hand, once Cenzo was in the truck, he might as well be locked in a safe for all the good he could do Giulia. Only he couldn't claim now to be a fisherman and offer the roughness of his hands as evidence. Damn.

"Excuse me. I beg your pardon. One phone call will straighten this out," Cenzo said.

"Get in line. Tonight everyone is calling Goebbels."

"If I can just show you my papers, which are all in order," Cenzo said. It was not true, but Cenzo was willing to say anything to buy time.

"What about her papers? Your sweetheart's."

"She lost them in a raid."

"Can she speak?"

"She's French."

"She's a little scrawny, but we'll keep her and let you go. How's that for a trade?"

"In fact, she is a favorite of the High Command."

"Is that so? Of the entire High Command? Does she have a special talent?"

Giulia had listened to the conversation but her eyes were brilliant and Cenzo wished she looked less interesting.

"*Je donne des leçons d'equitation au général Kassel*," she said.

Personal riding lessons for the general? That gave the sergeant all sorts of reasons to hesitate.

"Go," he finally said, "get the devil out of here."

Giulia was unprepared for Giorgio. Physically, the resemblance to Cenzo was startling, with the same broad features and dark eyes; but while Cenzo had a singularity, Giorgio had the smoothness of someone who had played many roles. He had been a navy frogman, a mountaineer, an Arctic explorer, a matinee idol, and more. He could play any number of leading men, but, maybe, with each role he lost a little bit of himself.

"Ah, the prodigal brother," Giorgio said. "I worried about you. Remember, I loaned you some of my best clothes."

"Don't worry about me," Cenzo said.

"Just keep your head down. I don't want any holes in my hats. Where have you been?"

"He was with me," Giulia said.

Giorgio studied her. "This is the fair Giulia? Cenzo didn't tell me you were so attractive. But I'm sure he's told you nothing good about me either."

"Maybe we should go someplace else," Giulia suggested to Cenzo.

Giorgio protested, "Maria would be very unhappy with me if I chased you away."

Giulia turned to Cenzo. "Is this true?"

"Yes."

"Maria Paz will be down in a moment," Giorgio said. "She is tending to her husband, who is ill. You can imagine the difficulties of transferring medicine and supplies in wartime, but she is ingenious. And she is fond of Cenzo. I can't imagine why."

They all turned as the gate to an elevator opened for a woman who was both mature and powerfully seductive.

"Welcome. I am Maria Paz Rodriguez and this is the residence of the Argentine consul. Please come out to the veranda. I wish I could offer you better hospitality, but all the china and glasses are packed."

"I'm surprised Otto and Vera aren't here," Cenzo said.

"My ever-present guests," Maria Paz explained to Giulia.

"More like stowaways," Giorgio said.

"I'm afraid that's what we're doing now," Giulia said.

"Nonsense, war makes us all equal. We're in the process of moving," Maria said. "Or is it ducking? Sit, please. Every day we have a different configuration of furniture and new ways to trip over it. How old are you, dear?"

"Eighteen."

"My God, that makes me feel ancient."

"She needs a passport," Cenzo said.

"What's the urgency?" Maria asked.

"Someone is trying to kill her," Cenzo said.

"Who?"

"We don't know. Her father was involved in negotiations for surrender and his group was betrayed."

"By whom? Can you point him out?" Maria asked.

"I would recognize him anywhere," Giulia said.

"Ah, I see the drink cart," Giorgio said. "A martini cannot be far behind. Cenzo, I know you would like to shoot me, but first we should celebrate. Some patriots from the navy came to see me. They wanted me to take a one-man submarine and sink a British battleship."

"You've done it before," said Cenzo.

"But I was younger then. Do you know how many men there are on a battleship? About a thousand. They wanted to sink the ship as a final gesture. I might have done it if there were a chance of winning, but now it's just murder. I'm sorry, I ramble on. So, to build a perfect martini: first, a martini glass of gin, then a discreet drop of vermouth and stir. Try it."

"No, thanks," Cenzo said.

"What a killjoy."

"The Germans are rounding up the Italian SS and shipping them to labor camps," Cenzo said.

"My heart bleeds for them," Maria said.

"And my news is that I've been fired," Giorgio said.

"You? The Lion of Tripoli?" Cenzo asked.

Giorgio swallowed his martini and cleared his throat to make room for another. "Maybe one of the ladies would like a drink? Yes, I'm a voice from the past. They're going to let a younger announcer try his hand. Less connected to the old regime."

"Who is 'they?'" Giulia asked.

"The propaganda office. The forces that be."

"Are they watching you?" Cenzo asked.

"What do you mean?"

"They fired you and let you walk away?" Cenzo asked. "I would think you know all sorts of embarrassing secrets. The emphasis on 'embarrassing.'"

"I suppose someone may be following me. Let them. I'm not going to spend my days watching my back."

"You're not afraid?" Cenzo asked.

"Let's just say I'll be on the alert. By the way, the bar has been open a full ten minutes and we have yet to see Otto and Vera. Not a good sign."

"And where Vera is you will find Claretta, and where Claretta is you will find Mussolini. No one has seen Claretta for days," said Maria. "Or Otto, for that matter."

"The war has yet to begin in Salò," said Giorgio. "Once the attack begins, partisans will go door-to-door hunting for Fascists."

"Won't that mean you?" Giulia had hardly spoken since she arrived at the consulate.

"You have an out," Cenzo said to Giorgio. "You were trying to help Colonel Steiner negotiate a surrender."

"That's not good enough for partisans like Dante," said Giorgio. "He demands a moral cleansing. What are you and Giulia going to do?"

"The best thing for us is to leave." Cenzo turned to Maria. "But she needs a passport. Can you make her one?"

Maria went into the reception room and came back with a passport. "The only problem is that I'm out of the passport business. In fact, I'm out of papers of identification altogether except for this one. Someone else's photograph is pasted in and she's not exactly Snow White." The picture was of a woman in her thirties who looked shrunken by grief, with gray hair and dark half-moons under her eyes.

"Can you do it?" Giulia asked.

"Can I turn a woman into a girl? It's easier to turn a fiddle into a priceless violin than to take the years off a woman's face. We'll see if I can perform a miracle."

30

Maria Paz sat in the basement of the consulate and rubbed the edge of the ID with sandpaper. Blew the dust off. Soaked the pages with watered-down coffee. Dried them with a hair dryer and used the picture's abuse to welcome old creases and create new ones.

Giulia sat on a stool next to Maria and followed her work. From time to time the girl glanced up at violins in different stages of creation; some instruments gleamed like honey, others looked naked without varnish or headless without scrolls.

"We'll lighten the face, darken the hair," Maria said, "and look for similar characteristics such as a beauty mark, passionate lips, an intellectual forehead. They swallow it every time. Since we don't want to leave paint on the surface of the print, we're using a pencil instead." She studied the photo from every angle as if it were a work by Leonardo. "Petty officials always sign with a flourish. It's their way of exercising power." She dipped her pen into a bottle of Pelikan ink. "How old are you again?"

"Eighteen."

"And how long were you with Cenzo on his boat?"

"Three weeks."

"And . . ."

"What?"

"Nothing happened? A man and a woman are alone on a small boat for three weeks and you tell me that nothing happened?"

"None of your business."

"Well, if I were alone with a man for three weeks on a small boat, he would know it. I'm sorry. I didn't lose my virginity, I sold it to the highest bidder. And by then I was already an accomplished forger."

"I don't think I'll need either skill."

"You never know. More importantly, I learned how to make men think they were taking advantage of me. You're not selling a painting or a violin, you're selling a story. 'Keep your head and you won't lose it' was my first lover's advice. He was French. Unfortunately, he lost his head to the guillotine."

"What about you and Giorgio?" Giulia asked.

"There's no denying that we've slept together, but we're grown-ups. It doesn't mean anything to him or me."

"It doesn't? What about Gina? Wasn't he in love with her?"

"Poor man. He had never fallen in love before, and I think for the first time in his life, he suffered."

While the two women worked downstairs in Maria's studio, Cenzo and Giorgio shared the consulate reception room like two snakes in a basket.

"You're having a grand time, aren't you?" Giorgio said. "Do you think you're going to be happy going back to Pellestrina now that you've seen the big wide world?"

"Don't worry, I'll enjoy watching you go under, then I can happily go back to fishing in Pellestrina. Out of curiosity, how did you lose your position of honor? If ever I saw someone who would eat worms for the sake of advancement, it would be you."

"You know, there were times when I actually missed having you around. Then I thought: No, I'd just as soon push you under a train." Giorgio tapped out cigarettes, one for Cenzo and one for himself.

Cenzo thought Giorgio was more worried than he let on. He had the expression of a man used to being in control but, without his position at the radio, how could he claim to be the "Voice of a New Italy"?

Maria Paz and Giulia brought wine and glasses up the stairs and Maria showed the ID to Cenzo. "Crude, but it will do. We have to let it dry anyway. The last touch will be the 'Aryan stripe,' " a red diagonal stripe on the photo page.

"You don't seriously think anyone is going to exercise the racial laws at this point," Giorgio said.

"Only a thousand SS at checkpoints," Cenzo said.

"And then what?"

"Then I will finally get back to the Lido and empty my nets. There must be a million fish in them by now."

"That's all you can think of?" Giorgio asked. "Catching fish?"

Cenzo hadn't meant it seriously, but now, having uttered the words, he understood how they could be misinterpreted.

"What will *you* do?" Maria asked Giulia.

"Yes, what will I do?" Giulia asked Cenzo.

He hesitated, because with Giulia every step could be a slip.

"I don't see you cleaning fish for the rest of your life," Giorgio said.

"It's not entirely up to me," she said.

Yet it sounded wrong, Cenzo thought, as if he were dismissing her, and she looked away. "I mean, she knows what she wants."

"Do I?" Giulia asked.

But she would be an outsider in Pellestrina, Cenzo thought. It was selfish of him to complicate her life. She could be a teacher or a tourist guide or just plain rich. He could only be a fisherman and the most he could hope for was to deliver her safely to Venice.

"She can make up her own mind. Giorgio is right," Cenzo said. "I think small. He thinks of the big picture whether he is with Mussolini or against."

"Should I take that as a compliment?" Giorgio asked.

"Not really. You know, I wondered whether you might denounce Il Duce on the radio. It would have been a brilliant stroke. Now that your radio career is *kaput*, you'll have to find something else to deliver. Maybe an American chocolate bar? Something."

To change the subject, Maria said, "I thought Otto might have joined Mussolini's convoy. The only thing I can't figure out is why. I've never known Otto to play with dice that weren't loaded in his favor. For that matter, why is Mussolini driving aimlessly around the lakes?"

"There's nothing aimless about it," Giorgio said. "He's visiting banks and picking up gold bullion as he goes. And who is better positioned to help with the swift deposit of gold into Swiss Banks than Otto Klein?"

"How can he do that?" Giulia asked.

"Who can stop him?" Cenzo said. "He's still Mussolini."

Conversation stopped at the sound of the earth being concussed.

"Good Lord, what was that?" Maria asked.

They ran outside to see black smoke climb the horizon to the north.

"The Garda Tunnel," Giorgio said. "The Allies are bombing it."

"No," Cenzo said. "There aren't any planes. The Germans must be setting off explosives to stop the Americans from coming through."

What were high explosives but innocent gasses moving fast enough to tear apart metal and flesh? Some soldiers sat by the road with blood caked around their noses and ears. Others wandered, stupefied by the sound of an explosion that continued to reverberate in their heads. There weren't as many flames as Cenzo expected; the force of the explosion had snuffed out most blazes. But a multitude of small fires hopped like living creatures from place to place, and as ambulances arrived, medics had to maneuver around twisted, unidentifiable pieces of artillery. The robot tank lay wrapped in its own loose treads.

Colonel Steiner was black as a coal miner but he stood at the mouth of the tunnel and directed a circus of litters and trucks, shouting over the sound of heavy machinery. His face and hands were charred from dragging bodies from the fire and his eyebrows were singed. Cenzo thought that when the colonel got to the hospital, they would have to peel off his clothes.

"What happened?" Cenzo asked.

Steiner said he didn't know. "I think a rocket launcher went off on its own. We still have more unexploded ammunition in the tunnel and at least one man alive."

Cenzo heard a muffled cry that seemed to come from the center of the earth. "Can you get him out?"

"The poor boy is trapped," Steiner said.

"That's going to drive the other men crazy," Giorgio said.

A soldier's nightmare was to die after hours of agony. Morphine, mother, and God were invoked, in that order.

"Have you tried to get to him?" Cenzo asked.

"Impossible. It's too unstable," Steiner said.

"Do you have morphine?" Cenzo asked.

Giulia read Cenzo's mind. "Don't do it," she said.

"I handled mines in Ethiopia. I'm used to this." Cenzo picked up a flashlight and a syrette of morphine from a medic, then tied a kerchief around his mouth and nose.

"You're not serious," Giorgio said.

"No," Cenzo said.

"You're not impressing anyone," Giorgio said.

"It's no worse than a dragon's asshole," Cenzo said to keep his spirits up and entered the cave. *All hope abandon, ye who enter here.* Cenzo had never appreciated Dante's Inferno so much.

As Cenzo entered, he saw no color, just the gray beam of his flashlight being sucked into a twisted maw.

"Can you hear me?" he shouted.

Cenzo knew land mines from his time in Africa. One type was as circular and heavy as a kitchen pot. A Bouncing Betty could bounce waist-high before exploding. The orange and green flags he had seen before had been blown away. He remembered that, as a general pattern, mines were planted every ten feet for tanks and every four feet for personnel. Theoretically, once a man knew the pattern, he could survive. Cenzo shuffled forward, the better to nudge land mines aside rather than step on them.

He crouched under the smoke and at points crawled rather than crouched. The explosives he used to know had been set to detonate in a sequence; this one had been detonated like a single lightning bolt.

"Hello?" Cenzo called, but sound was absorbed and there was no response apart from a cry farther on. The trick was not to get trapped by will-o'-the-wisps that danced among the cartridges; he had to beat out flames that started to crawl up his pant leg.

"Can you hear me?" Cenzo called again. He squeezed between the tank and a tunnel wall, both hot from the blast.

The cries stopped directly in front of him and the flashlight found the bright eyes of a man on the point of death. Cenzo felt the tunnel shift around him. The soldier was a boy and he pointed to his belt. *Gott mit Uns* was engraved on his buckle. *God Is with Us.*

Cenzo crawled closer and released the buckle. The soldier's relief seemed exquisite, then his intestines poured out, his head lolled to the side, and he was dead.

"Jesus," Cenzo said. He couldn't imagine what kind of God would mete out such agony.

"I've seen worse," a voice said from behind.

Cenzo twisted around.

"Giorgio?"

All Cenzo could see of his brother was his head. In the close beams of the flashlights, it was like sharing hell with the devil.

Blood was everywhere. Religious medals hung around the necks of dead Polish workers, Iron Crosses on German sappers.

Cenzo sneezed and the tank suddenly began to move. It had a comic aspect, like a funny man's double take, but the top tread caught his pants and dragged him slowly but single-mindedly forward. A Panzer tank weighed about forty tons. It was not an equal match, but Giorgio tried to jam pieces of metal he found into the track without losing a finger.

"Have you ever played three-card monte?" Giorgio asked.

Cenzo nodded.

"Did you ever win?" Giorgio asked.

"No."

"Well, this time you have to win."

Giorgio scampered away. On his own, Cenzo felt the ponderous force of the tank as it crushed the tunnel's floor.

"Still there?" Giorgio reappeared with a crowbar, a mere toothpick compared to the Panzer; but when he inserted it between two of the tank's interlocking plates of armor the beast came to a shuddering halt, rocked back, released itself, and came to a standstill.

Cenzo leapt out of his pants and rolled away to the mouth of the tunnel.

"That was fucked," he said.

"Doubly fucked." Giorgio bent over laughing. "I've never seen a man get out of a pair of pants so fast in my life."

They brought the soldier's body with them as they backed out of the tunnel. The scene looked less like a battlefront and more like a medical unit. In the noise and confusion, Giulia barely looked up from the tourniquet she was tying to the leg of a soldier.

"Tell me, Cenzo, is the war over for this boy now? Do you have to find more bodies?" she asked.

"He knows what he's doing," Giorgio said.

"No he doesn't. He has no idea, any more than this boy does. How old do you think he is? Sixteen? Seventeen?"

"Fifteen," Steiner said. "Cenzo, put on some shoes, please, and, Giorgio, find Mussolini and tell him that we have lost our escape route north."

"You mean, find the German army," Giorgio said.

"There *is* no more German army. Get to Mussolini. He'll recognize you."

Giulia said, "We should take you to the hospital. You're wounded too."

"And abandon my men? Some are still missing," Steiner said.

"You're crazy. God has forgotten them," Cenzo said. "He has no idea where they are."

31

For twenty years the grandees of Italian industry had prospered as partners of Il Duce. Now they lined up their cars on the Salò golf course waiting to be rescued, to be lifted into the air out of harm's way. Mussolini himself was cosseted with Claretta in the backseat of a bulletproof Mercedes and guarded like Humpty Dumpty by a score of German SS. It was unclear whether they functioned as bodyguards or held him under house arrest.

Cenzo and Giulia watched from the far side of the Salò golf course as Giorgio failed to deliver Steiner's message. He approached group after group and was rebuffed time after time. Eminent financiers and respected industrialists were ready to show their leader they were loyal to the last. No one, however, wanted to be the bearer of bad news, and no one had told Mussolini about the explosion at the tunnel.

The Salò airstrip was an undulating fairway that had been overwhelmed by weeds. It was small, a nine-hole golf course, two hundred meters across the fairway and another ten meters across the green. Soldiers were posted along the perimeter of the field. They ignored the presence of Giulia and Cenzo as part of a bizarre Italian scene.

"How many passengers can go?" Giulia asked.

"They all think they're going," Cenzo said. "That's why they don't want to cause any trouble. They don't want to lose their seat. If the Germans send a nice fat bomber like a Junker, they can stuff it with about twenty passengers. Two Junkers, forty passengers. The alternative is a recon plane like the Stork that only carries two passengers, three at the most." Often with Mussolini, Cenzo had the sense not so much of a well-run operation as of a traveling circus.

"What makes them think there will even be a plane?" Giulia asked.

"They have no choice but to believe there will be. It's a matter of self-delusion."

"What is going to happen if a plane doesn't come?"

"Then he'll be trapped here in Salò."

Mussolini better hope that the American Ninth Army reached him before the partisans did, Cenzo thought. The Sherman tanks of the American Ninth Army might be blocked by the tunnel, but Dante's partisans could swarm in overnight.

"I don't see your brother," Giulia said.

"He's probably talked his way into the clubhouse. He's good at that sort of thing."

Mussolini stepped out on his car's running board to shout, "So the Germans blew themselves up at the Garda Tunnel. There's German efficiency for you. The obnoxious boasting we've had to endure." Mussolini puffed up his chest and crossed his arms as if he had scored a major victory. It was a pose that had hypnotized Italy for more than a dozen years. "The world will be astonished and those who betray Il Duce will be hung by their tails like rats."

There was always the promise of a new weapon. A giant rocket. A superbomb. A jet plane that could sweep up everything in the air. Cenzo had listened to this sort of Fascist spiel most of his life and he still found it breathtaking in its insanity.

When the day grew dark, Il Duce, Claretta, Vera, and their inner circle of Fascists retreated to the airstrip's old clubhouse, entertaining themselves with descriptions of how they would take revenge on deserters. The Germans, meanwhile, camouflaged their trucks, ate spartan rations, and filled up jerry cans with petrol.

Late into the evening, Mussolini and Claretta reenacted Napoleon's escape from Elba. Marshal Ney had promised to bring Napoleon back to Paris in an iron cage, but he could not resist the call of his former emperor when Napoleon declared, "Soldiers, your general, called to the throne by the choice of the people and raised on their shields, has come back to you." Then Napoleon opened his famous greatcoat, stuck a red, white, and blue cockade in his hat, and declared, "Let him among you who wants to kill his Emperor, fire!"

"Not a shot was fired," Claretta said with well-practiced awe.

What was not mentioned was that Napoleon's escape route had ended at Waterloo.

Cenzo and Giulia melded in among the birches. She interlaced her fingers with his. "I remember the first time I touched your hands, thinking how hard they were. Do you remember how we danced for shrimp? I was sure the Germans were going to fire at us."

"You showed great promise at fishing and dancing."

She dropped his hand. "Such a sad story about the girl and the fisherman. You said it was up to me whether I stayed or not. Maybe I would have preferred that you told me to stay."

"You would go crazy living in Pellestrina. I don't want to watch you go crazy."

"You're right. Life would be a little dull."

Cenzo was trying to think of a rejoinder when someone stepped out of the trees behind him and the loop of a garrote fell around his neck, not hard enough to draw blood but with enough tension to keep him still.

"Be quiet," the Spaniard whispered.

"I *am* quiet," Cenzo said.

"The girl?"

"I'm quiet too."

The Spaniard slipped the garrote off Cenzo. He seemed genuinely relieved he didn't have to pinch Cenzo's head off. "Is this the girl you were looking for? She won't scream and run about like a chicken?"

"She won't."

"That could lead to dire circumstances for everyone."

"This is my friend," Cenzo said, introducing Giulia to the Spaniard.

"Friend? Hard to say. It's not so much that you're a dishonest man as that you're a bad liar."

"Is that what you came to tell me?"

"Dante has changed his mind. He doesn't want Giorgio dead. Not yet, at least."

"What does he want?"

"He wants your brother alive."

"Really?" Cenzo asked. "Isn't a dead Giorgio Vianello what every partisan prays for?"

"I wouldn't know. I'm an atheist."

"So why has Dante changed his mind?"

"You shouldn't ask so many questions." The Spaniard rolled up the garrote and stuffed it in his jacket. "I like you in spite of yourself. Why are you still here? Go back to Pellestrina. By tomorrow, Mussolini will look like an old sock and you will, too, if you're with him. You don't want that to happen."

"Not me," Cenzo said, but the Spaniard had already slipped into the dark.

32

At midnight, the trucks lined up crosswise and illuminated the airstrip with headlights as wide as baking pans. A perfect night for flying. Mussolini stepped out of the clubhouse into a welter of light. Cenzo thought all the scene needed was a roll of drums and wondered what an Allied plane passing overhead might think. Perhaps a late-night round of golf? The lights were doused and better aligned. Then turned on again.

A faint buzz trimmed the treetops and a plane not much larger than a toy hung in, and touched down at the end of an aerodynamic swoop. No German or Italian plane wanted to be in the air for long. The pilot executed his landing in less than ten seconds, bounced up the ninth fairway, and rolled to a stop. He pushed open his side panel and jumped to the ground. He was the same pilot whom Cenzo had seen on his previous visit to the airstrip with Otto and it was the same recon plane, a Stork.

Mussolini stepped forward, received the pilot's salute, and magnanimously announced that the bond between Italy and the Third Reich would never be broken. He declared he would fight to the bitter end and that other, larger planes would arrive soon. No one believed him, but what choice did they have?

At this point events started to move quickly. Bars of gold were carried from the clubhouse to the plane. Mussolini climbed into the Stork. Standing by a wing, Claretta closed her eyes and crossed her fingers. There had been talk about flying her out with Mussolini; plainly, she had been replaced by more gold. It was the same model Stork that had earlier rescued Mussolini in the Alps and Il Duce had all the faith in the world in it.

The pilot removed the parking chocks, delivered two counterclockwise turns to the propeller, jumped in his seat, and discovered that much of the space around his feet was now taken up by loose bars of gold stamped "99% Pure London Good Delivery." Mussolini pulled on his helmet, and dismay spread among his true believers. The dashboard trembled. The engine revved. There was little point in reaching for radio contact, since there was no German or Italian radio to make contact with. Cenzo caught sight of Otto Klein in his trademark white suit and remembered Maria's description of him as a ringmaster of fleas. So he had gotten this far, but what did he plan to do?

The pilot shouted over his shoulder, "Too much weight." It was an embarrassing miscalculation. He handed down a dozen gold bars, and the plane waddled goose-fashion to the top of the fairway. As Mussolini, a Man of Destiny, stood up to give a valedictory wave, the plane's windshield cracked around a bullet hole. One shot caught the pilot and he rolled off the wing onto the ground.

Other bullets whistled past. Once the Spaniard fired, other partisans began sniping. German soldiers hustled Mussolini to his Mercedes. The Stork continued to roll forward in neutral, its propeller a blur, while Cenzo ran to the Stork and climbed in to apply the brakes. Giulia ran after him and nimbly climbed through the struts like a child on monkey bars.

The plane bounced along on donut tires and

gathered momentum as it reached the downslope of the fairway. Otto Klein ran along Giulia's side of the plane, holding a gun.

"Now you will halt!" Otto demanded. This was a new, more assertive film producer.

"Don't stop!" Giulia yelled over the sound of the motor. "It's DaCosta!"

"Otto?" Cenzo revved the engine and the plane leapt forward. There was confusion on the ground about whether to fire or not; no one liked to see bars of gold waltz out the door.

"You will stop!" said Otto. He grabbed a wing, but the plane wasn't nearly as fragile as it looked and kept on rolling.

From the cockpit box, Cenzo took a thick-barreled flare gun and handed it to Giulia. A phosphorescent flare burned at thousands of degrees.

"Shoot him!" Cenzo said.

Giulia kicked the window flap open and fired. Otto ducked and let go as the flare hissed on a red line straight up to the sky.

33

It had been a long time since Cenzo piloted a plane and the air that streamed through the bullet hole in the windshield tasted cold and fresh. He stayed close to the ground and watched Allied bombers pass far overhead on their way to the railroad junctions of Verona. There was not much left to bomb and no opposition.

Giulia hovered in the green light of the instrument panel. "DaCosta would have killed us both."

"I bet there isn't anyone in this war that wouldn't like to kill us. Allies, Germans, Fascists, partisans. What do you want to do with all this gold?" Cenzo asked.

"I don't know. What do you want to do with it?"

"Well, we could head toward Switzerland. I hear they have a high regard for the stuff."

"Seriously?"

"I don't know. I only intended to stop the plane, I didn't mean to steal it."

"Did you see Giorgio?" Giulia asked.

"Not once the plane started to roll."

"He was shooting at the partisans, I think. It was hard to say which side he was on."

"That's often the way with Giorgio."

Bits of glass blew off the windshield frame. The wet footprints of Lake Como and Lake Maggiore passed below while the plane dropped and bounced back.

"This weather is getting nasty," Cenzo said.

With so much gold, Cenzo had to fly full throttle to keep from stalling. Altogether, between ingots in satchels and ingots loose on the floor, the Stork could be carrying as much as six hundred extra pounds. There had been no time to properly stack and tie down the bars. When the cargo shifted, the entire plane swung from side to side.

"We're too heavy," he told Giulia. "I don't have enough control or altitude. We have to dump some weight."

"How much?"

Cenzo felt his mouth go dry. It was too painful to contemplate. "How much gold do we have?"

"About twenty bars, I think."

Cenzo glanced over his shoulder. The gold gleamed like beautiful fish. "Start with two."

She opened the window flap and pushed out two gold ingots, watching them plunge one by one into the dark. Cenzo felt the plane float upward, then drop like an elevator.

"More," he said.

Giulia lifted two more bars. They dropped like golden tears.

Soon the plane was swinging low over Venice, a small corner of the Mediterranean. A hundred heartbeats more and the plane crossed from one side of the island to the other. He passed over the old madhouses on San Servolo and San Clemente, the hospital that Giulia had escaped from. Fishing boats were dots of light on the surface of the lagoon.

Cenzo had not attempted to land a plane in years. The plane's speed and pitch gauges were no longer functioning, the altimeter had started to drop, and the crosswind be damned.

"All the rest," Cenzo said. "Dump all the rest."

The plane was low enough now to see the bars plunge into the water. Cenzo reminded himself: Level out. Flare. Touch down. He hoped he wasn't forgetting anything. He cut the lights and the Stork descended into the dark, aiming straight for the breakwater. He cut the engine and glided silently over the village of Pellestrina, too low to use parachutes and too high to jump.

"Do you have any idea where we're going to land?" Giulia asked.

"I have an idea. It shouldn't be more difficult than parking a car."

Cenzo pulled the plane's nose up.

"Hang on," he said.

"What does that mean?"

"It means hang on."

Cenzo wasn't trying so much a landing as a controlled stall. The plane was no better than a glider now, and the thing about gliders was that there were no go-arounds. At the last moment he turned on his lights and passed over nets hung on poles and dinghies deep in water. Giulia bent over in her seat and prayed, "*Merda, merda, merda.*" Cenzo was running out of anywhere to land when the Stork plowed through the wooden stakes of a vegetable garden and crashed into a potting shed, the impact cushioned by a trellis of grapes.

His head ringing, he opened his eyes and looked over at Giulia. Her head tilted to one side, her hair covered her face, and blood ran down her forehead. Cenzo unbuckled his straps so he could loosen hers and he caught her as she fell forward.

He leaned her back and pressed his bandana against her forehead. She opened her eyes. "Did we land or did we crash?"

"A little of both," Cenzo said. "Are you okay?"

"I'm a little dizzy."

Nido emerged from the bar wearing a nightshirt and carrying a flashlight. He walked up to the plane and peered in.

"Cenzo? Is that you?"

"It seems so."

"Did you intend to land in my garden?"

"More or less."

"Who's that with you?"

"Giulia. Can you help me lift her out?"

They carried her into the bar and gently stretched her out in a booth. Cenzo was unable to look away from the blood that outlined her cheek.

"She got the air knocked out of her," Nido said. "I've seen it happen in the ring a hundred times. She should sit up and breathe deep. Once you clean up the scratches she'll feel a lot better. I'm just wondering why you chose to land a plane in the dark. Dare I ask, is anyone chasing you?"

"Everyone is . . . after Cenzo," Giulia said.

"Do you think you can move your arms and legs?" Cenzo asked her.

Giulia nodded. "Are you hurt?" she asked.

"Barely a scratch."

"Life is unfair that way," said Nido. "I have found a little grappa improves almost any situation."

"Water even would be nice," Giulia said.

Nido poured water for Giulia and grappa for Cenzo and himself. He felt benign and Cenzo felt enormous relief. Cenzo held the glass of water while Giulia lifted her head to drink.

"But why a German plane?" Nido asked.

"It was spur-of-the-moment," said Cenzo.

"I'm sure it was. What are you going to do?" he asked.

"Disappear," Cenzo said.

"And the plane? Is that going to disappear? Everyone will know that you left Salò and ended up here in a German plane," Nido said. "That makes you a marked man. And me, too, since you landed in my garden."

"I'm sorry about that," Cenzo said.

"These things happen." Nido became solemn. "You swore you would stay out of trouble."

"I tried," Cenzo said. "God knows, I tried."

"I have to get dressed," Nido said. "It's going to be a long day. You know, I've spent a lifetime in this bar telling lies about prizefights and foreign lands. This is the first time I've ever had a story like this to tell, and it's too much. Nobody will believe me."

"And the gold. They'll never believe that," said Giulia.

Nido lifted his head ponderously, as a great turtle might. "What gold?"

"Don't worry," Cenzo said. "We dumped it. It was too heavy."

"Too heavy! You stole a plane full of gold and dumped it?"

"Yes."

"Do people think you still have it?"

"Probably."

"And you came here? I almost feel like a rich man."

With each detail, the story got worse.

"And what about *her?*" Nido gestured to Giulia.

"She's with me."

"With you? This sounds like more than a complication," Nido said. "Aren't you supposed to be getting married to Celestina at the end of the war? That's what your mother says. She says it would solve all your problems, respectability being the biggest, apparently."

"No, the biggest would be being married to Celestina."

"But you promised 'at the end of the war.'"

"I thought Mussolini would hang on a little longer." Cenzo's body was starting to stiffen up from a multitude of bruises. He stood up and walked outside.

Dawn was rapidly changing color from gun-metal gray to flamingo pink. Fishing boats bobbed on the water. A chubby boy, the Son of the She-Wolf, stood in Nido's garden. He was absolutely still, transfixed by the wreck of the Stork.

34

With daylight, the children of Pelestrina gathered around the plane like witnesses to a miraculous apparition, running their fingertips over bullet holes, peering through the shattered windshield, racing under the plane's wings. The Stork was a phenomenally reliable aircraft, served by oversized wings that could spread like a vulture's or fold like a cicada's.

Cenzo disengaged the propeller from the grapevines it had nested in. "It's a miracle we didn't break our necks. I'm sorry about your garden."

"You landed where you landed," Nido said. "The question is, how you are going to get it out of here?"

Cenzo knew that he needed to reach the road and, to do that, he had to squeeze between the garden and the shrine. Once on the road, he would have to avoid potholes to gather speed.

He had never paid much attention to the shrine at the end of Nido's garden. It wasn't much larger than a bus shelter, a whitewashed hut dedicated to Our Lady of Fatima. From there he had thirty meters for takeoff before he hit the water.

But they weren't going anywhere. What was the old saying? Cenzo thought. "So near and yet so far"? For all their running, they were back where they had started, in the devil's vest pocket.

"Who is the boy?" Giulia asked.

"The Son of the She-Wolf, although he looks more like a small bear," Cenzo said.

"He's our squadron leader's boy," Nido said. "His name is Umberto."

"You think he's a spy?" Giulia asked.

"I don't know," Nido said. "I would have said yes, but I find that he's developing new tastes. Yesterday I caught him reading comic books behind the bar."

"Everything is changed," Cenzo said.

"Everyone—the Germans, the partisans, and the Fascists—thinks you have the gold," Nido said. "How many bars of gold do you think you threw out of your plane?"

"Maybe twenty," Giulia said. "Maybe more."

"Makes me shiver," Nido said.

"The problem is that in their minds we still have a fortune in gold," Cenzo said.

The ancient pensioners, Enrico and Salvatore, ventured up the street like a pair of well-dressed crabs. "Do you have any nets for us to mend?" Enrico's eyes darted to the plane.

"This has every element of insanity a man could hope for," Nido said.

"Ha-ha. It only gets better," Salvatore said.

Out of breath, Sofia Vianello appeared close behind. "Cenzo, how long were you going to wait to tell us? You don't come home and then you don't tell us when you do. Do you know how insulting that is?"

Celestina followed with eyes narrowed to slits.

"Hello, Mama," Cenzo said, and set the propeller on the ground.

"Why do you call me your mother? Is this how a son treats a mother? You think the neighbors don't notice?" Indeed, heads leaned out of doorways the length of the street. "And who is this?" she added, indicating Giulia.

"This is my friend."

"A girl?"

"That's right."

"How old is this girl?"

Giulia said, "I'm eighteen."

Sofia turned to Giulia. "Eighteen? You're married, I presume."

"No."

"By eighteen, most girls are married." Sofia acknowledged the airplane poised at the edge of Nido's garden. "Where's your brother? You didn't fly here yourself."

"He's still in Salò, as far as I know."

"Not one good word to say for your older brother, who probably saved your neck. Meanwhile poor Celestina has to wait and wait." Sofia seemed to become aware of her neighbors hanging on every word. "Vianellos do not conduct family matters in the street. Come home and have some breakfast."

"Maybe Giulia can come too? She especially likes your polenta."

At the kitchen table, Sofia offered stale biscotti and espresso. Giulia declined both. She took in the kitchen of dark wood and copper pots hung according to size. In general, the furniture had the sort of earnest, oppressive quality that drove men to their boats.

Sofia asked Giulia, "Your family are not fishermen, are they?"

"But she can fish," Cenzo said.

"Cenzo can fish on his own," Sofia said. "He's a good provider when he remembers his family comes first, or he's not distracted by every giddy thing that comes his way."

"Like the war?" Cenzo said.

"We are going to marry as soon as the war is over," Celestina said. "That's the agreement."

"The family has an understanding," Sofia explained to Giulia. "I lost my youngest boy, Hugo, Celestina's husband. I received a medal as a Heroic Mother."

"Pinned on her by Mussolini himself," Celestina said.

"And Cenzo agreed to take Hugo's place," Sofia said. "Really, all they need is a priest and a registrar."

"I don't think the war is over quite yet," Cenzo said. "There are still some holdouts. There's plenty of fighting left."

"We'll see." Sofia offered Giulia a cookie. "Why don't you sleep here tonight? We'll say you're a cousin. Cenzo can stay at his shack. I think that's best."

"This is Pellestrina," Cenzo said. "Everybody is related to everyone else. We will fool no one."

"Still, it's a matter of your reputation. If not your reputation, then your friend's. What will people think of a girl who spends her nights with a man who is engaged to be married to another woman?"

"Maybe that she's a deckhand?" Cenzo said.

"You're not serious. See, Innocenzo, I know you better than anyone else. You made a death-bed promise to your father, whom you loved. You would never break such a promise."

"If I'm just a deckhand, I don't think it matters where I go," Giulia said.

"See, she agrees." Sofia slapped her hands together now that she finally had the conversation on the right track. "I'll make polenta for breakfast and she can go to church with us."

"Even if I'm Jewish?"

"We'll make an exception." Sofia wasn't fazed. "Like the pope."

35

For two years Venice had been a cowed and crowded city, intimidated by curfews and the policeman's rap on the door. On Liberation Day, a new Venice rose up despite the presence of Fascist snipers on rooftops. Partisans fought back with rifles that were handed from canals to palace windows. They tied red kerchiefs around their arms and waved the flag of the winged lion above St. Mark's Cathedral. Some whores proved to be patriots. Women who had taken Germans as lovers had their hair brutally cropped by the partisans. Mussolini himself had been spotted by a partisan who shouted, "Hey, here's Big Head!" He was executed against a stone wall with Claretta, his lover, who had been loyal to the end.

The day of liberation was followed by days of uncertainty. Whoever had been on top was likely to find himself on the bottom. Not only soldiers and Fascists had to adjust, but also the technocrats and bureaucrats who had kept the cogs of the state turning, switching portraits of Il Duce for the pope. Some prisoners had to stay behind bars no matter what. Others were prisoners in the morning, partisans at noon, and government ministers by evening. And vice versa. It was hard to say who was more vulnerable, the famous or the anonymous, although it was generally agreed that big heads rolled best.

Cenzo waited for some form of authority to appear in Pellestrina, much the same way he expected Giulia to disappear at any moment. What was an educated, beautiful person like her doing with him? She could tie any variety of knots and tell jokes in three different languages. She even made him feel irrationally optimistic, and that surely was against the natural order of things.

Peace had been kind to Colonel Steiner. He could have been placed in a prisoner-of-war camp; instead he was hospitalized in a Venetian palazzo decorated with murals of Romans resting on cushions and eating grapes. The doctors came by twice a day and nurses lubricated his burns with salve.

He peered through bandages and spoke in a raspy voice. "Americans respect rank. They give us everything but slippers and bathrobes. Prisoners of war are expected to work, but they're paid for it and the higher ranks don't have to work at all."

"So you're comfortable?" Cenzo asked.

"Except that I feel like a mummy. The doctors encourage me to move around, so there is an element of discomfort, but it's for my own good. I never could have afforded such luxury before the war." The colonel peered over a windowsill at the guard post below. "Is that Giulia Silber, by any chance?" A week had passed since the crash of the Stork, and except for a bruise on her forehead it was almost unnatural how rapidly she had recovered.

Cenzo nodded. She could have been a student engrossed in a book, although he knew her concentration was entirely on his meeting with Steiner. She glanced up and flicked her hair over her forehead. "The guards allow you only one visitor at a time. Otherwise she would have come up."

"I remember her from the tunnel. She had nerve."

"She still does. When do you expect to be released?" Cenzo asked.

"It's up to the doctors and then the judges."

"What will you do then?"

"I was thinking of writing my memoirs before amnesia sets in. There will be a nationwide amnesia, wait and see. What is the young lady going to do now? Leave Italy?"

"I have no idea." It was something he had tried not to think about. "She's an intellectual. She can argue with anyone about anything."

"I know her parents are dead, but maybe she has other relatives that can help her out?"

"There aren't many relatives left," Cenzo said.

"I think some Jews in Italy got away. At least I hope so. I know that more than two hundred were sent to the camps from Venice and eight thousand from Italy. This isn't Poland or Germany. Would you mind lighting a cigarette for me?" Steiner asked. Cenzo lit one and Steiner took a luxurious draw that ended as a wracking cough.

"There's something I wanted to ask," Cenzo said. "Was it an accident?"

Steiner gave him a questioning look. "What?"

"The explosion at the tunnel. At the time, you thought it might be a matter of sabotage. Do you still think so?"

"Maybe. There will be an inquiry. I know I never did anything that a soldier couldn't do with honor intact. You yourself understand the efforts I made for a German surrender. Do you want to know what I dream about? Skiing. I dream about skiing on a slope of absolutely pure snow. My wife and son are right behind me and I hear the sound of their skis and we simply never stop. But it's a dream."

Cenzo could have left it at that and walked away. If there was going to be an inquiry, wouldn't there be an investigation?

"Do you remember the SS raid on the hospital of San Clemente?" Cenzo asked.

"You mean, where I saw a ghost run down to the water?"

"It wasn't a ghost," said Cenzo. "It was Giulia. You and Lieutenant Hoff were in a gunboat looking for her."

"Hoff was. He had a list."

"But there were two conspiracies, the Silber Ring to end the war and the Hoff Ring to keep it going and kill as many Jews as possible. The Silber Ring never had a chance, did it? Not really."

"Overall, I'd have to say that is correct."

"Which means that Giulia's father never had a chance. He was just played for a sucker."

"You could say so. I met with Silber and his group for about a year. Usually I reported to General Kassel. Silber had the business connections and General Kassel offered the prestige of the professional soldier. But the plans were leaked; they generally are if they sit on the shelf too long. It was more a matter of bad timing. Six months before was too early. The Germans weren't ready to quit. Six months later they were ready, but we had been compromised. The Americans came up with basically the same unconditional surrender, but with different players."

"Nobody warned Silber's ring, did they?" Cenzo said. "Because they still played a part."

"What are you suggesting?"

"I'm saying that since Silber's cards were already on the table, the Allies pretended to use them," Cenzo said. "They led him to believe that his plan was still operational. Is that what made him so effective as a decoy?"

"He was a diversion," Steiner said. "Switzerland was full of spies and decoys all watching each other. The more spies that wasted their time watching Silber and his friends, the fewer watched the Allied forces. There are always decoys. Before the invasion of Normandy, the Allies filled the channel with plywood boats and cutout soldiers."

"When did you hear there was a raid at the hospital?"

"Hoff told me that night. That's why he was celebrating. He was proud of himself for scooping up the last of the Jews."

"He didn't know that you were part of the Silber Ring?"

"No, otherwise I would have been picked up."

"No offense, but what could you provide?"

Steiner said what was self-evident. "What do you think? The Garda Tunnel."

"To provide an escape route for the Germans or block the Americans?" Cenzo asked.

"It's a matter of timing, isn't it?"

So the puzzle was still incomplete. Cenzo looked down at a line of German soldiers in uniform being force-marched by partisans along the canal.

Steiner took in the same spectacle. "I heard that some SS were weighted with cobblestones and thrown into the water."

"There are always rumors like that at the end of a war," Cenzo said.

"There are also fantastic stories about Mussolini's gold."

"And then there's the man who betrayed the Silber Group, DaCosta," Cenzo said. "He's like a cat that wanders in and out of rooms."

"Did you find him?" Steiner said.

"We saw him in Salò. He goes by the name of Otto Klein and claims to be in the film business. I'm sure he still wants to see Giulia dead."

"Then what I would do, if I were your friend Giulia, is get out of Italy as fast as possible. And if I were you, I would accept that the war is over. We should all carry on as best we can and get on with normal life. I heard you crashed a plane in Pellestrina. Surely, that's not normal."

Normal life? What was that? Cenzo wondered.

Sailing back to Pellestrina, Cenzo reported to Giulia everything Steiner had told him, with one exception. He didn't think it was necessary to pass on a description of Vittorio Silber as a decoy, a mere dupe for German intelligence. Her father had given his life bravely. From here on, Cenzo wanted her to concentrate on saving her self.

"Do you believe Steiner?" Giulia asked.

"Yes and no. He lied to me. He tried to convince me that Russo was dead. I think he's honest to a point."

She shot him a sideways look. "That's not very helpful."

"I think he's trying to keep his honor intact, which is not easy for a German officer these days."

They sailed in silence for a while. She brushed hair out of her eyes and he impulsively kissed her.

"Why did you do that?" she asked.

"You looked available."

She kept her eye on him and laughed. The truth was that he felt that soon she would not be available and he found himself starting to store memories.

Out of nowhere, Giulia asked, "Where do you think Giorgio is?"

"I have no idea."

"And you don't care."

"That's right."

"Did you always hate him?"

"We used to be best friends. But that changed."

"You don't seem so upset with him now."

Cenzo realized it was true. He was like a man who awakes and finds his fever had broken.

"I'm not jealous now," said Cenzo. "But we have always been competitive."

"In what way?"

Cenzo thought for a minute. "Do you remember the amusement park on the Lido? It had a Ferris wheel and a roller coaster, but its main attraction was a metal cage that a motorcycle daredevil would ride inside of, wearing a white scarf. He went round and round and reached a vertical orbit, a true 360 degrees. At the end, he would climb down and dare anyone in the audience to match his feat. No one was expected to step forward. Giorgio not only accepted the dare but rode the machine like a pro, wearing the white scarf and all. When he stepped off the bike, he passed the challenge to me and personally tied the scarf around my neck. I didn't have a choice. 'What have you got to lose?' Giorgio asked. I did fairly well, but on the top of my third spin the scarf got caught in the front wheel and about screwed my head off. I learned a valuable lesson. You always have something to lose."

36

Giorgio must have known he would be arrested or worse by the partisans in Salò. The only place that the Lion of Tripoli was welcome was Pellestrina, the fishing village he had left years ago.

Cenzo watched him take long walks along the seawall. They had been solitary strolls to begin with, then accompanied by Umberto, the former Son of the She-Wolf. The boy walked beside Giorgio and whipped the air with sea grass.

"Umberto won't talk to me," Farina told Cenzo. "He blames everything on Mussolini."

"A lot of people do," Cenzo said.

"He and his friends do nothing but hang out at the plane in Nido's garden."

"Well, it's not going anywhere," Cenzo said.

But within days Cenzo and Giorgio began to work on the Stork. The war had littered Italy with the husks of plane crashes and the Americans were especially profligate with their postwar refuse. To begin with, the two of them plus Giulia and Umberto rolled the plane back. They had to turn the plane around to face the road in a space that seemed impossibly tight. To do this, they unlocked the wings at their roots, slid them back like insect wings, and rolled the plane through the vegetable garden, then spread the wings again and locked them into place.

Giorgio hoisted himself up through the pilot's side flap to examine the instrument panel. "It could be worse. The turn-and-bank indicator, the altimeter, attitude, compass, and airspeed gauges, are busted. But the fuel looks good and I don't smell any leaking gasoline, and that's a definite plus."

Cenzo inspected the plane's body. "We have at least six holes in the fuselage, a twisted aileron, a snapped tail skid, and a hole in the windshield."

Giorgio flicked the on/off switch and the airplane's engine hiccupped. "Also I'd say we're close to empty."

"Look!" Umberto pointed up in the sky to a floatplane towing a red and white banner that said Coca-Cola. It circled over them. Somehow it didn't look friendly.

"Americans." Giorgio followed the plane with

his eyes. "They don't miss a trick. Umberto, a quiz: What do you think was the last German plane to see combat? Would you say a big, powerful bomber?"

"I suppose so."

Giorgio connected wires to gauges. "Wrong. Would you say a fighter plane?"

"I guess so."

"No, not even a Messerschmitt would have dared in the last days. The last German plane in the sky was undoubtedly a Stork just like this, sent on a rescue mission to hell."

"How are you going to fix all the bullet holes?" Umberto asked.

"Patch and paint," said Cenzo. "That will be your job. It's not difficult. Pretend it's a sail."

Umberto could have been knighted for the honor he felt.

The work went swimmingly until a plume of dust approached from the road.

"Maybe you should go inside for a while," Cenzo said to Giorgio.

"Police?" Giorgio asked.

"Worse. Partisans." Unsaid was the knowledge that police arrested, partisans shot.

A black Fiat came to a stop and the Spaniard and his protégé Peppino emerged. The war was barely over and the Spaniard already looked as if he missed it. His beret was beaten and dusty and his eyes looked as if he hadn't slept in days. Peppino let a tommy gun hang casually around his neck.

They walked around the plane as if visiting a pair of harmless lunatics.

"We heard about this," the Spaniard said. "Peppino didn't believe me, but I said that crazy man Cenzo Vianello will try anything. I saw him fly away like a saint ascending into heaven with much more than fish in his hold. Now here you are with your brother Giorgio, working on that same plane. But why? Why would two brothers, who by all accounts hate each other, put so much effort into a plane that cannot fly? Where do they want to go? Incidentally, where is the girl who was with you at the airstrip in Salò?"

"I don't know," Cenzo said. "She went off on her bicycle."

"Then it's up to you. Where is the gold?"

"There is no gold. We threw it out of the plane. It was too heavy."

"It was too heavy! *Jesu*! Those should be the words on your tombstone." The Spaniard rubbed his face. "That isn't the answer I need. Not at all." He noticed Umberto standing on the fuselage with patches of fabric in one hand and glue in the other. "And who is this?"

"This is our master mechanic," Giorgio said.

"He looks more like a house painter. Come on down, *chico*, where I can keep an eye on you."

"Stay where you are," Cenzo said.

"Why are you making this difficult?" the Spaniard

asked. He kicked a rutabaga. "This garden really is a mess."

"When people start landing planes on your vegetable garden, everything is turned upside down, rutabagas be damned," said Cenzo.

The Spaniard laughed and turned to Giorgio. "And you're just going to fly away in this wreck?"

"It's going to fly like a bird," Umberto said.

"I'm sure it will someday," the Spaniard said. "And someday we all will be angels in heaven. I used to be a partisan, now I'm an undertaker. So!" A pistol dropped from the Spaniard's sleeve into his hand. "Come on, Giorgio, let's take a walk, you and I. A last stroll for two old warriors. I have no orders concerning Cenzo. He and Peppino can stay here with the kid. And as a matter of professional courtesy, I can offer you different manners of execution. With or without a blindfold. Guillotine, garrote, bullet, blade, poison, or suffocation. Standing, sitting, or on your knees."

"That sounds like a menu," Giorgio said. "How about a plane crash? I could die in the crash of my own plane. I don't mean a skid, I mean a real catastrophe."

"Unfortunately, I have orders."

"Aren't you tired?" Cenzo asked.

The Spaniard slumped. "You have no idea."

"I know you would never accept a bribe," Giorgio said. "I wouldn't ask you to. A donation is different."

"How is that?"

"With a bribe, money goes from one hand to another. With a donation, money goes to heaven."

"You mean the Church? Too bad, I'm an atheist."

"All the better. You can claim a miracle anytime you want."

"How big a miracle?"

"That's up to you," Cenzo said.

"I want the gold I came for. Tell me how many bars you and your girlfriend flew off with."

"I have no idea how many we left with," Cenzo said. "But as I told you, we had to throw them out of the plane."

"Just tell me how many you ended up with!"

"None."

"One bar," Umberto corrected Cenzo. "It fell under a seat on the plane."

Amused, the Spaniard asked, "And where is that one?"

"Follow me," Umberto said. He led the way to Our Lady of Fatima and opened the door of the shrine. The interior was lit by a single votive candle and a bar of gold that shone like the sun.

37

"I'm not sure I'd be so easy to defend in court," Giorgio said. "I'm not a war criminal, but I couldn't exactly call myself a war innocent."

"He was sent to execute Giorgio," Cenzo said. "Among other things."

"I had the impression that the Spaniard was someone who rarely left empty-handed," Giulia said. "How did you get rid of him?"

"We gave him a bar of gold," Giorgio said.

"Where did you get that?" Giulia asked.

"Umberto found it under a seat in our plane," Cenzo said. "He found it the first night. It turns out that he's more religious than any of us knew."

Umberto nodded vigorously, taking it as a compliment.

"So there's nothing to worry about."

"Not quite," Giorgio said. "The Spaniard says there are more men on their way. I'm going to be snatched. Not arrested but snatched off the street as a radio war criminal like Lord Haw-Haw or Axis Sally."

"They can't do that," Giulia said.

"They're the power now," Cenzo said. He noticed that the basket on her bike was empty. He thought she had been shopping. Had she met an American officer who happened to be an expert on Byron? There were any number of possibilities, but it seemed ungrateful to question her when here she was, standing by his side.

As if reading his mind, she said, "I went to see my old house. It was too sad."

"I'm sorry," Cenzo said. "We'll go back together and find out what's happened to it."

She wiped her eyes and blew on the pinwheel Cenzo was holding.

"This is our makeshift aerometer," Cenzo said.

"You don't mean to take off today?" she asked Giorgio.

"Why not? I have a good headwind. And it sounds as if I'll have company pretty soon." He smacked the fuselage. "I just need ten seconds to clear the houses."

"Why only ten seconds?"

"The lighter the plane, the easier it is to get airborne. We've stripped it down to nothing."

"Will the propeller stay on?" Giulia asked. "Seriously. Half your instruments are broken."

"You know, at this point, they're pretty much advisory," Giorgio said. "If I just reach the sea I'll be fine."

"Which sea?"

"Whatever comes first."

"When will you go?" she asked Giorgio.

The brothers looked at each other.

"I think now is an excellent time," Giorgio said.

"Will it fly?" Giulia asked.

"Theoretically." Giorgio climbed into the pilot's seat.

Cenzo performed a walk-around inspection even as they traded thumbs-up. He wound the propeller two times counterclockwise while Giulia removed the chocks and ran out of the path of the plane. Giorgio hit the ignition switch and the engine came alive, wheezing smoke. Umberto saluted and the plane rolled.

At ten seconds, the plane bumped over rough ground and potholes. At eighteen, Cenzo watched his brother pull back on the stick, too soon for an ordinary plane. The Stork climbed straight up, nearly tipping backwards, and seemed to balance on its tail. Heads peered out bedroom windows and ducked inside as the plane skimmed rooftops, then straightened out and aimed for the blue horizon.

38

Cenzo rowed the dinghy to Pellestrina and what loomed like a moon on the horizon was Celestina waiting to claim her due. He wondered what he would say to her, now that he understood the painting of the three brothers, of the youngest trying to drown the oldest. Hugo had idolized Giorgio. In a way, Giorgio had not been able to resist his own charm. Women took pride in flirting with a famous actor and Celestina was no different. She telegraphed her sensuality, which was no small weapon. Hugo would still be sailing the *Fatima* and joking on deck but for Celestina.

What a fool Hugo must have felt, as had Cenzo before. At least between Giorgio and Gina there had been genuine emotion, small solace for the cuckold. With Celestina, Giorgio had been playing with a toy.

There had been no official celebration of the liberation. Days had built up to a spontaneous joy. Now boats lined up along the dock and as good as breathed to the same rhythm. Cenzo didn't want Giulia to suffer more questions from his mother, so once they reached the dock he dropped her off at Nido's and went on to his mother's house. Sofia and Celestina met him on the doorstep.

"Tell him," Sofia said.

"Tell me what?" Cenzo asked.

"Celestina doesn't want Giulia at the wedding."

"It's not as if she's family," Celestina said. "She's just going to raise questions, don't you think?"

"I think you're right," Cenzo said. "There's bound to be curiosity."

"And it will be a small wedding because it is my second and it's wartime." Celestina made it sound patriotic. "We don't want to make too much of a fuss."

"Let's take a walk," Cenzo said.

"You just got home. Where are you two love-birds going?" Sofia asked.

"Just for a stroll," he said.

"That's romantic," Sofia said. "Don't stay out late."

The waterfront almost had a carnival air. The Germans had decamped and taken their detested blackout with them. Someone set an old gramophone on a chair and cranked out music on 78s. "*Baciami! Baciami!*" Children celebrated by staying up late and running up and down the dock with paper cones of shaved ice and cherry syrup.

"Would you mind if I got an ice?" Celestina asked.

"Go ahead."

"So warm, like summer." She returned with the ice and gave him a coquettish look over her shoulder.

Cenzo brushed off a bench for Celestina to sit on.

"This must be serious," she said.

"It is."

"I've never heard you be serious." She giggled. Her lips were a bright red from the cherry ice.

"Do you think Giorgio should be at the wedding?" he asked.

"Why shouldn't he be?"

"Because he slept with the bride."

Celestina was thrown into confusion. She half

stood and craned to look in the direction of Sofia's house. "That's not funny," she said finally.

"I didn't think so either."

"Who told you that?"

"Who could?"

"Giorgio? He lied."

"The Lion of Tripoli lied?"

"There's a misunderstanding."

"Well, he'll be arriving any day now. We can ask him together."

"It was a long time ago," she said.

"While you were married to Hugo."

She sank back against the bench. "Giorgio wanted to give me a screen test."

"Did he?"

"We started out that way. Hugo caught us."

"So you didn't make a screen test for Giorgio," Cenzo said.

"Not a real one."

"What does that mean?"

"Pictures. Completely innocent, most of them."

"You're dripping." Cherry syrup spotted the front of her dress.

There was no denying that Celestina was deflated. One minute she was a desirable widow, the next she was a woman scorned.

"It's that girl, isn't it?" she asked.

"Giulia? She's after the fact."

"What do I say to your mother?"

"Tell her the wedding is off. The rest I leave up

to your imagination." He was starting to feel sorry for Celestina. "Look, I'm already a scandal. You can do better. Scarpa, for example. I bet you can snare him before the night is out."

"He's always hanging around," she admitted.

"That's the spirit."

39

Ordinarily the bar was exclusively male. On this night of all nights whole families crowded into Nido's establishment to celebrate. The old fishermen, Salvatore and Enrico, cadged drinks and sang a toothless "*Baciami! Baciami!*"

"You look happy," Cenzo said to Nido.

"Why shouldn't I be? The bar is crowded and there's money in the till." Nido put a glass in Cenzo's hand. "And soon I will have fuel for my beautiful motorboat. Do you know what Americans like to do? They like to race back and forth on the lagoon. How would you like American whiskey for a change?"

"Why not? Have you seen Giulia? We were supposed to meet here."

"I saw her a few minutes ago but she left." Nido lifted his glass. "To Giulia, your will-o'-the-wisp."

"What do you mean?"

"I mean, don't let your heart get broken again. I'm speaking as a friend."

Scarpa of the *Barking Dog* elbowed his way to the bar. "Let me tell you, Cenzo, I've never seen a prettier deckhand than yours. Aren't you still engaged to Celestina?"

"I think she's interested in someone else."

"A lucky man," Scarpa said, and moved on.

Cenzo looked over the crowd and saw Otto in a far corner. His was an interesting disguise, that of a buffoon in a white suit.

"I'm taking some provisions from the back room if that's all right with you," Cenzo told Nido.

"Provisions for what?"

"I may be gone for a day or two," Cenzo said.

The village's promenade was packed with married couples strolling arm in arm. Songs drifted in the dark. Giulia must have seen Otto too. She had the ability to fold into shadows when necessary.

It was, however, ex–squadron leader Farina who emerged from the shadows. No longer dressed in a Fascist uniform, he was like a priest without vestments. He dragged Umberto, his son, by the arm.

"Where are you going in such a rush?" Farina asked.

"Taking the air." Cenzo tried to slide past.

"I doubt it. You're always up to mischief."

"Why don't we talk about my mischief another time."

"Everyone in Pellestrina thinks you're some

kind of hero," Farina said. "I know you're nothing but a thief. Umberto saw you give a gold bar to the partisans."

"No I didn't." Umberto snatched his hand away and ran.

"There goes your witness," Cenzo said.

"It doesn't matter, I will denounce you. You will tell the authorities what you did with the rest of it."

"What 'rest of it'? I don't have any gold," Cenzo said. "And what authorities? Italian? American? Partisan? Maybe an unpopular Fascist would make a better suspect. In any case, no police are here yet, are they?"

Farina tucked his head between his shoulders and walked off.

Cenzo made his way to his dinghy but Giulia was nowhere in sight. He looked over the water and saw a splash that was too far out for any ordinary swimmer. He rowed with a single oar, first on one side, then the other.

As he approached, Giulia stood waiting and the miserable little shack looked like paradise.

40

At dawn the *Fatima* sailed past decrepit channel markers that leaned together like conspirators. Giulia held a lantern at the bow as the boat heaved on the breast of each wave, and when the lagoon became too shallow, Cenzo raised the rudder and lowered the sail to pass through the channel's twists and turns.

The lagoon was variably a cake of mud, a screen of reeds, or a maze that twisted back on itself loop after loop, becoming smaller and smaller, from *sacco* to *sacchetto*. At low tide, they got out together to push the boat toward the dock of a deserted crab station. They were wet enough for their clothes to cling to their skin, and in the light of the lamp Giulia was transformed into a fierce little sea nymph. Cenzo was so distracted that he rammed the boat into the dock. Cats abandoned on the island mewed in self-pity.

"Where are we?" Giulia asked.

"One of my father's favorite fishing stations. There's a reason why the fish gather. It's the mouth of a stream or it's where currents come together. You can't see them but they do, and even underwater they can carry you." He jumped onto the dock and cranked an extra-wide net into the water. "We're fishing the clouds with the most beautiful net in the world."

"You told me before."

"By the time we return, the net will be full. The main thing is to keep your hat on and your dignity intact. Nobody wants to wear a wet hat, as my father used to say."

"Will DaCosta find us?"

"In time. It all depends on how smart he is. If

it's just him, not in a million years. If he enlists a fisherman as a guide, in a few days. And . . ."

"And . . . ?" Giulia prompted. "You were about to say something else."

"We'll see."

" 'We'll see' is a very annoying answer. It's what grown-ups say to their children."

"You're right. The sun is up."

As it rose, the sun cast silhouettes that crept across the water. When the *Fatima* began moving again, Cenzo moved to the front of the boat to part willow boughs.

"What was your father like?" Giulia asked.

"My father? There's not much to tell. He was a fisherman. Giorgio called him 'simple.' "

"Was he?"

"No. My father wasn't an educated man but he was what could be called a 'natural philosopher.' A bit of a dreamer. Sometimes he didn't catch as many fish as he should have because he was so busy watching the world. He could tell you when a kestrel was about to dive or how a duck's wings drummed against the water. It was a mystery to him how nature could be so evenhanded and how the ugly and the beautiful could trade places. Some fishermen tossed dynamite into the lagoon and brought hundreds of fish to the surface. They were thugs, not fishermen. It wasn't the illegality that bothered my father so much as the affront to nature. One night the thugs were visited by Enrico Vianello. He demanded respect for fish. Obviously, he was crazy. Can you believe it? Respect for fish?"

"What did they do?"

"They beat the hell out of him, naturally. But from then on they left the fish alone. That was what my father considered a worthwhile trade." Cenzo pointed out a yellow snake squirming like a ribbon on the surface of the water. "This part of the lagoon used to be owned by duck hunters," he said. "Long ago it was a route of the Roman Empire. A person could walk through history on such a road."

As they passed some reeds, he drew Giulia's attention to a shotgun four times the size of an ordinary weapon.

"A *s'ciópon*," he said.

"I remember," Giulia said. "It sounds like an assassin's weapon."

A *s'ciópon* was a boat. It was also a shotgun. It was built for a hunter to lie in and slaughter as many as fifty ducks with a single shot. Cenzo opened a waterproof bag of tools he had brought from Nido's. He broke open the barrel and reamed the inside with rag, rod, and turpentine. It was a prehistoric weapon, at least a hundred pounds in weight plus a pound of black shot, with a recoil that could break a shoulder. It was like cleaning the teeth of a monster.

"You came prepared," Giulia said. "Who is that for?"

"I'm not positive. Taking no chances."

When he was satisfied that the gun was clean, he loaded it with a heavyweight two-gauge cartridge and laid it behind the duck blind.

"Happy?" Giulia asked.

"I'm getting there." They returned to the *Fatima* and punted from one narrow channel to another. The Marsh of Centrega ran into the Marsh of St. Gaggian which ran into the Marsh of Tralo and on and on. Over the course of the night, Cenzo had set one *s'ciópon* and two cloud nets at different locales. It wasn't like laying mines in Abyssinia, but close enough.

"My father said that if he ever wanted to, he could hide out in the lagoon for a hundred years."

"Was he a better fisherman than you?"

"Easily. The only fisherman who rivaled the old man was Hugo. Hugo had a gift."

"And Giorgio?"

"Giorgio doesn't have the patience for fishing. He's a lion, remember."

Evening brought swallows darting through the air. As the channel widened with the tide, the *Fatima* shifted under a stand of mangrove trees. They left the boat tied up, carried their food and canteens, and waded knee-deep in the direction of another fishing shack. There was no sign of recent use or habitation. They climbed moss-covered stairs up to a rough deck with loose boards. Inside were nets, crusty pans, and sardines that only a fisherman would consider sufficient for existence. Rusted spears and shovels stood in a corner. Post-cards of the Virgin were tacked to the wall.

"The place has a rustic quality," Giulia said.

"Are you superstitious?" Cenzo asked.

"No," Giulia said.

"Good. Then we can stay here tonight."

Dinner was biscuits washed down with the tinny taste of canteen water. They lay on the deck and watched a full moon slip from cloud to cloud. Cenzo didn't think of the past or future anymore, only the present.

"You know what we did for fun?" Giulia asked.

"Quoted poetry?"

"Raced cars."

"You're not serious."

"My father's company sponsored racing cars. Have you ever driven a car at a hundred miles an hour?"

"No."

"You ought to try it."

"I will."

"What did you mean by asking if I was superstitious?"

"Nothing," Cenzo said.

"Don't be a tease. Is it a ghost story?"

"It's not quite a ghost story."

"Go on."

"Okay. Years ago, there was an exceedingly beautiful woman who lived on the Lido and dealt in black-market cigarettes. Naturally she was envied, and one day she disappeared. People said she had struck it rich or run off with a sailor or entered a convent. All sorts of crazy ideas. The police gave up after a week, but then some boys who were swimming in this part of the lagoon pulled a steamer trunk out of the water."

"With the woman in it? I know how these stories usually go."

Cenzo continued. "The woman was in the trunk, chopped up and covered with squid and crabs. She had been killed by a blow to the back of the head and dismembered, limb by limb. The boys ran home with arms full of squid and crabs only to discover that the squid had the eyes of the dead woman. Since then, most fishermen have stopped fishing here. At least for squid."

"And on windy nights, does she moan?"

"Of course," he said.

"And were the killers caught?"

"There were two. One was lost at sea and the other went insane. But as I said, it's just a ghost story."

She asked, "Are you superstitious?"

"Very. Every fisherman is."

"Are you trying to scare me?"

"Just a little."

Light retreated from the lagoon in a blink. They listened to water slap against the deck.

"Sometimes I have the feeling that I'm Alice and I've gone through the looking glass," she said. "Only I'm not following a white rabbit, I'm following a mad fisherman who leads me on wild escapades and has a circle of friends and family each more lunatic than the other. Are they as dangerous as he makes them out to be? I can't tell. I probably should escape, and yet I can't. I'm his prisoner."

"I have nothing to offer you," Cenzo said, "except a boat."

"You have ghost stories."

"And polenta."

She lifted herself up onto one elbow. "Is this a game?"

"No, it's not a game."

"That's what I thought." She traced his mouth with her fingertip. "You know more about the world than I do."

"The lagoon I know."

Cenzo was silent for a long time.

"I'm sorry," he said.

She rolled close enough to let their bodies touch. "What for?"

"I'm not going to wait any longer." He kissed her.

"You don't have to."

She lifted her hips and let him slide off her pants, at which point they might as well have been going a hundred miles per hour.

41

They woke at the sound of a Stork outfitted with pontoons flying in and out of channels, looking for enough clear water to land on. When the plane banked, Cenzo could make out Giorgio in the green glow of the cockpit light.

"Who is it?" Giulia asked.

"Giorgio's flying. I didn't get a look at the others."

"Do you think they saw the boat?" Giulia asked.

"I'm sure they got an eyeful."

"Then I'm staying with you," Giulia said.

"They'll shoot us both. If I can't defend my lagoon, I don't deserve it. Don't you think there's something Byronic about that?"

"So you're a romantic after all."

The Stork flew out of sight.

"You have to go," he said. "It will be back. Don't show yourself, no matter what." He gave her a kiss and a push and she slipped into the eelgrass.

Cenzo lit a cigarette and waited. Two hundred meters on, the Stork executed a tight and perfect turn. Following its searchlight the plane dodged rocks and branches and touched down in the dark as lightly as a dragonfly. Cenzo had to admire the touch of a master.

In a moment, flashlight beams reached into the dark. Farina stepped onto a pontoon and sank to his knees in swamp water. It didn't faze him because he had returned to dressing in Fascist black. Otto Klein in his trademark white suit bulled his way through the water and up onto the dock of the shack. Cenzo was disappointed to see his brother consorting with lowlifes like Otto and Farina. He was almost nostalgic for the heroic Lion of Tripoli.

"Two Vianello brothers. What are the odds on that?" Otto asked.

"In the Venice Lagoon, pretty good," Cenzo said.

"Excellent point," Otto said. "We're just a search party. There's no reason for anyone to get hurt."

"They needed a pilot who knew the ins and outs." Giorgio sounded unapologetic.

Cenzo turned to Otto. "So you were play-acting in Salò."

"I played the fool. Now the play is over."

Ex–squadron leader Farina patted Cenzo down for a gun and took the opportunity for a shove. "Give me your knife, the one you gut fish with."

Cenzo handed over a broad-bladed knife. "How proud do you think your Son of the She Wolf would be if he could see you now?"

"It's the way of the world. He had to find out sometime."

Cenzo noticed that all three carried guns. "You look more like an invading army than a rescue party."

"Volunteers, I assure you," Otto said. "The squadron leader was especially keen on joining us, but we don't want to linger. Where's the girl?"

"Gone."

"You mean gone into hiding," Otto said. "Oh, I bet you could lead us on a merry chase in and out of this swamp if you wanted. Like Tarzan of the Apes swinging on vines. But I doubt our little Miss Silber will venture far from you."

"You're not going to find anyone in this swamp at night," said Giorgio.

"Well, there are two ways to catch a mouse. Chase it or let it come to you." Otto held his pistol straight up and fired a round that punctuated the dark. The sound of the shot resonated through the trees. "It's simple. If the girl doesn't care for Cenzo, she will keep on running. If she does care, she will return."

"She'll run," Farina said.

"For some reason, I don't think so," Otto said. "In the meantime, why don't we see what's inside the cabin?"

Eager to please, Farina climbed the stairs and shined his flashlight beam around the interior of the shack. There were nets, fishing gear and, as luck would have it, a dead squid curled up in the bottom of a bucket.

"Okay, the girl is gone for now," Otto said. "So where's the gold?"

"What gold?" Cenzo asked.

"We know you have it," Farina said. "My son found a gold bar you let a partisan walk off with. As his father the gold goes to my protection."

Cenzo turned to Giorgio. "What are you doing with these thieves? You were free and clear. Why didn't you walk away?"

"Not free and not clear. Life as a target is no fun, no fun at all."

"In films this is called a Mexican standoff," Otto said. "No one walks away."

Dark kept progress to a crawl. Cenzo led Farina, Giorgio, and Otto on a trail that was barely visible. He had decided on a route that would swing by the *s'ciópon*. They stumbled through a marsh that was solid one moment and muck the next. From time to time Cenzo thought he heard an extra footfall and sensed that Giulia was keeping pace. None of them could see beyond the person ahead, but night was giving way to the dawn even as they walked.

"You know what's really insulting?" Otto said. "The Allies didn't bomb Salò, not once. They blew up soldiers the length of Italy, but Mussolini was not worth the expenditure of a single bomb. I feel for the suckers who volunteered. They wanted to die for the Motherland. Well, they got six feet of it." Otto laughed. "Remember how

Mussolini asked women to donate their wedding rings for the war effort? 'A proud and moving sacrifice by the women of Italy,' he told them. Melted down it added up to tons of gold."

"You might want to hurry," Cenzo said. "You never know when an American fighter plane might spot us from above and wonder why a German plane is hiding in the lagoon."

Cenzo heard something drop in the water. Farina felt around his feet.

"I dropped my gun."

"We're not going to wait for you," Otto said.

"Just a second, please."

"If we leave you behind, there's no gold for you."

"Always the optimist," Cenzo said. "More for you and Giorgio, right?"

"Did you ever get a little bit jealous of your brother?" Otto asked Cenzo. "Was he always the leading man, the hero?"

"Maybe. But would I trade places with him? No."

They were nearing the *s'ciópon*. Slogging through the marsh was hard work, and Otto let Farina catch up. "Did you find your gun?"

"No."

"We should make you walk with your boots off. In fact, we'll let you go first," said Otto.

The channel widened and narrowed according to its whim, but the tide was definitely going out, exposing more and more of the channel. Cenzo saw the muzzle of the *s'ciópon* poke out of the reeds. Farina, marching at the head of the column, saw it first. He lifted the barrel but couldn't control the weight of its stock, and by the time he cocked and pulled the trigger, its momentum carried his aim well off target. The shot went off with the force of a small artillery piece and sprayed enough buckshot to knock Cenzo to the ground.

"Cenzo!" Giulia called.

"I'm okay! Stay down!" Cenzo yelled back.

"Get the girl!" Otto ordered.

Cenzo crawled in the direction of her voice. As long as they were in the dark, they were relatively safe, but the night was fading fast and light was spreading. Giorgio had not spoken or fired his gun and Cenzo wondered if he had been hit.

Otto called, "Giulia, Giulia, where the hell art thou?"

Cenzo heard a triumphant "I got her!" from Farina and turned around to see Giulia staring at Otto as if she had seen a ghost or a ghost had seen her.

"DaCosta," she said.

"You can call me Otto."

"I can call you whatever I want. Your name was DaCosta when you murdered my parents."

"Frankly, my dear, no one gives a damn."

She tried to slap him, but Otto caught her hand.

318

"That's all you can say? Did you watch them die?"

"No, but there's a sameness in death. I can assure you that they were dead before they hit the ground."

"Shut up, Otto," Cenzo said.

"Brave talk for a man without a gun," said Otto. He grabbed Giulia and twisted her arm behind her back. "So if there is any gold, lead us to it. If not, I can shoot her now and they'll find your bones with hers a year hence and declare you—the Germans have a word for it— *kaput*."

"Not yet," Giorgio said. He limped into view, bloodstains covering one sleeve.

"What happened to you?" Farina asked.

"What happened?" Giorgio said. "You almost killed me with that fucking cannon, you idiot!"

Farina protested, "It was an accident."

"Are you in any condition to fly a plane?" asked Otto. "I've been holding your brother Cenzo in reserve if you can't. In compensation for your pain and suffering, we'll give you one of his bars of gold. Or we can flip for it."

"I have a favorite coin," said Giorgio.

"Of course you do," Cenzo said. "And a lucky pack of cards or lucky dice. The problem is there's no gold."

"What do you mean?" Farina asked.

"There's no gold. I told you before."

"But I saw a bar with my own eyes. There has to be more," Farina said.

"You're suffering from wishful thinking," Cenzo said. "Gold has that effect."

"Keep moving," Otto said.

As the group pushed through the swamp, insects vibrated with silvery wings and the air took on a languid warmth.

Otto asked idly, "Didn't we pass the same willow before, or is that an illusion too?"

"All willows look alike," said Giorgio.

"Why aren't you more upset?" Farina asked Otto.

"Because Otto doesn't care," Cenzo said. "If we found gold, that would be nice. It would make him rich. But what he really needs is to get rid of witnesses like Giulia. Otherwise it's the gallows for him."

"Why?" Farina asked.

"Because he's a war criminal and she can testify against him."

"Giorgio," Otto said, "if I asked, could you put a bullet through your brother's head? Would that shut him up?"

"I'm sure it would. Except only he knows where the gold is, if there is any gold. I think we're about to find out."

They had arrived at the old crab station with its winch and pulley on deck. Cats came onto the dock to inspect the visitors. Crabs scuttled out of open crates. The sun burned its way onto the horizon and turned the surface of the water into a golden scum.

Otto looked at the net that covered the bottom of the channel and turned to Giulia. "This is your last chance. I saw you fly from Salò with a fortune in gold."

"We threw it off the plane," she said.

Triumph spread on Otto's face. "I think that's the most perverse thing I ever heard."

Otto raised his gun. "It's underwater in wooden crates," Cenzo quickly said.

"That's an improvement." Otto let go of Giulia. "See if it's down there," he told Farina.

"What do you mean?" Farina said. "I can't swim. Never have."

"I don't care. Get in the water and bring up the damn gold. Do it. And Cenzo, get away from the winch."

"Do you know much about fishing?" Giorgio asked.

"No."

"I didn't think so."

Cenzo cranked the winch, doing what fishermen did when they fished the clouds.

Giorgio, with his good arm, grabbed a rope.

Giulia dove into the water. Otto was startled and moved along the dock to shoot her when she surfaced, but she swam in and out of shadow and gilded scum. Cenzo couldn't tell at what point he and his brother had decided to work together, at the last moment or from the start, but the four corners of the net lifted and became a single shimmering cloud floating in the air. Otto looked up as the net swung directly overhead and Giorgio pulled the rope that seemed to release all the fish in the sea.

42

Strange things happened at sea. How, for example, could the Swiss filmmaker Otto Klein slip and break his neck and drown on a dock piled high with fish? Or a corpse join the living at dinner? Or the dead whistle on empty bottles? And how could a squid flash the eyes of a dead woman?

Strangest of all, Cenzo thought, was the sight of a woman fishing. Giulia had become skilled. When a sea bass slipped its hook, she plunged after it. She could stir the sand and make a flatfish magically appear, and when she caught a goby in its tunnel, she did so with the élan of a cardsharp.

She couldn't leave and she couldn't stay. To claim her home, banks in Venice demanded that she provide a death certificate for parents killed in a concentration camp.

"The bastards!" Giulia said.

"You know you can quit fishing whenever you

want," Cenzo said. "You'd be a lot more comfortable anywhere else."

"You want me to quit?"

"No, I don't want you to quit, but there are other things you could be doing."

"Like what?"

"Translate, write, teach poetry."

"Escape to another life like Giorgio?" Giulia asked.

Cenzo didn't even know if Giorgio was alive. All he knew was that his plane had been found in Zurich, so he had gotten pretty far. Cenzo liked to imagine his brother as a croupier.

What was it about memory? Cenzo thought. So often you only understood how you felt about someone after they were gone. The scale had finally tipped and Cenzo found himself forgiving Giorgio. His brother was a badly flawed person but, on balance, he was also Prince Charming. That was his fate.

There was something tragic about Maria Paz and her husband the consul, one vibrant and the other slipping away like a boat on the edge of the water. Farina had a lesser fate, searching for gold ingots that appeared and disappeared like worms in the mud.

The distant whistle of a railroad train signaled that it was time for Cenzo and Giulia to get their catch to market. She watered fish under sailcloth while he set the sail.

"Maybe I'll apply to university," Giulia said.

"If that's what you want."

"You know what I want?" Giulia asked. "I want to know whether or not you care if I go or not."

The sails of the *Barking Dog* and the *Unicorn* parted as the *Fatima* approached the dock of the Rialto and transferred baskets of sole and silvery *branzini*. As soon as money changed hands, the *Fatima* pulled away.

"Well?" she asked.

"You don't know? I can't live without you."

Giulia trailed a hand in the water. She allowed herself a smile.

"That's a start," she said.

The Grand Canal had already recaptured much of its old lights and sparkle. It was a mere façade in that many of the city's wartime refugees had left Venice as soon as it was liberated. Fair enough, Cenzo thought. The *Fatima* was a lifeboat that had served its purpose.

Its sail filled and snapped smartly as the boat hit open water and Venice drifted away.

ACKNOWLEDGMENTS

The sort of story I write is a creature that is half fiction and half fact. Or a kind of fiction designed to tell the truth. Or you could simply say I throw a wide net. The result is a profound thanks due many generous, blameless people.

In Venice I owe Fabio Carrera, Alberto Bullo, Gianfranco Bonesso, Bepi Rossi, Marco Borghi, Erla and Lino Zwingle. In Salò, Giancarlo Cipiani and Professor Antonio Arrigoni. In Pellestrina, the fishermen Giovanni and Roberto Mucciardi and Gianfranco Vianello, captains of their fate.

In London, my dear friend and agent, Andrew Nurnberg. In New York, my editor, Jofie Ferrari-Adler, who forgives all but bad prose. In California, Nell and Nelson Branco and Luisa Cruz Smith for their close reading. Don Sanders and Sam Smith for their patience. Bill Hanson for his Burmese python.

I can never adequately repay my fellow travelers Francisco and Barbara Aguilera, and Mark and Elizabeth Levy, or the best and most tireless of guides, Laura Sabbadin, who kept us from being lost in so many ways.

Although being lost in Venice is not the worst of fates.

ABOUT THE AUTHOR

Martin Cruz Smith's novels include *Tatiana*, *Stalin's Ghost*, *Gorky Park*, *Rose*, *December 6*, *Polar Star*, and *Stallion Gate*. A two-time winner of the Hammett Prize from the International Association of Crime Writers and a recipient of Britain's Gold Dagger Award, he lives in California.

Center Point Large Print
600 Brooks Road / PO Box 1
Thorndike, ME 04986-0001 USA

(207) 568-3717

US & Canada:
1 800 929-9108
www.centerpointlargeprint.com